Jean Wells
Buttonhole Stitch Appliqué

C&T PUBLISHING

Edited by Barbara Konzak Kuhn

Technical editing by Sally Lanzarotti

Design by Jill K. Berry, Artista

Watercolor illustrations © 1994 Rose Sheifer

Line drawings by Rose Sheifer

Pattern drawings by Janet White

All photography by Ross Chandler, Bend, Oregon.

Library of Congress Cataloging-in-Publication Data

Wells, Jean
    Buttonhole stitch appliqué / by Jean Wells
        p.   cm.
    ISBN 0-914881-91-4
    1. Appliqué—Patterns. 2. Quilts
    3. Wearable art. I. Title
TT779.W45   1995
746.44'5—dc20   94-38701

DMC is a registered trademark of the DMC Corporation.

Warm and Natural is a registered trademark of Warm Products

Fray Check is a trademark of the Dritz Corporation.

Offray is a brand name of C.M. Offray & Sons, Inc.

Velcro is a registered trademark of Velcro USA, Inc.

Published by C&T Publishing
P.O. Box 1456
Lafayette, California 94549

Printed in Hong Kong

10 9 8 7 6 5 4 3

Table of Contents

Acknowledgments

My wholehearted thanks to:

Jackie Erickson who stitched for me, and told me "yes, that looks good" or "no, it doesn't work." Thank you for the birdhouses and button bracelet.

Lawry Thorn who designed the angel doll and helped with the machine quilting.

Ursula Searles who helped with the buttonhole stitching.

Andrea Balosky who did all of the hand quilting on the quilts.

Barbara Slater who stitched bindings.

Ross Chandler who again photographed beautifully all of the projects.

Barbara Konzak Kuhn who helped develop the manuscript, and made sure everything was correct and attractive at the same time.

Diane Pedersen who oversaw the book design and contributed creative ideas for the look of the book.

Todd Hensley who believed that I had a good idea. Thank you for your never-ending encouragement and support.

Introduction

Buttonhole Stitch Appliqué is a book full of whimsical appliqué quilts, quilted banners, clothing, and simple crafts. The designs on the quilts are very playful. I sometimes call them quilted banners because the lively designs give them a banner appeal. Most of the fabric colors are bright and rich, and the embroidery thread further outlines and highlights the appliqué shape. The simplicity in design of Americana folk-art appeals to me, and the designs in this book remind me of this folk-art style. The projects are some of the funnest I've made, and I hope they bring you as much cheer.

After I made the first quilt, *Blackberry Pie* (page 30), I fell in love with the buttonhole-stitch technique. I like having work that can be done away from the sewing machine. This appliqué technique is very portable. Once a block is fused, you can carry it around with a bag of thread and stitch wherever you may be. Of course, if you want to buttonhole stitch on the machine, you can do

that also. All the projects' edges are finished with either hand or machine stitches.

The first chapter—Getting Started—instructs you on choosing supplies and fabrics. You will learn the ins and outs of buttonhole stitch appliqué and gain some tips on working with paper-backed adhesive. The project chapters begin with a quilt, then the quilt theme is carried through to related projects. Some of the accessories include a delightful bracelet of buttons and safety pins, a sewing caddy with its own needlecase, and a quilter's journal for your memorabilia. I try to inspire creativity by showing how easy it is to take a motif from a banner and use it to add whimsy to a child's coat or a fisherman's shirt. Most of the clothing items are purchased pieces where only the appliqués have been added. I enjoy giving presents and there are many gift ideas for you to use—on almost every page you turn.

Enjoy your quilting experience!

Choosing Supplies

Fabrics

I use 100% cotton fabrics in most of my quilts and quilted banners. Needles flow easily through pure cotton, making quilting fast and easy. Cotton fabrics vary in weight from quilting cotton (broadcloth weight) to corduroy to lightweight denim. The fabric yardage listed in the supply sections for the projects is based on a 42" width of fabric. Pure cotton is flexible and has a comfortable feel to it, so it's great for making garments. I made two of the garments with wool. I like using boiled wool or wool melton because the cut edges don't unravel. Because wool is often thicker than cotton, you can position the stitches further apart and the fabric won't distort. Plus, quilting through wool is like quilting through butter.

For the most part, the appliqués I've added to the projects use small pieces of fabric. Start collecting fat quarters

(18" x 22") or small cuts of fabrics in a variety of textures, colors, and styles. You will find it easier to start a project if you have a collection, because you'll have a variety of fabric choices. Most manufacturers add

sizing to new fabrics, so it's important to pre-wash and press cotton fabrics first, before using them, to remove the sizing. Wash wool by hand with a companion cleanser in cool water, or have it professionally dry cleaned. Of course, if you are using scraps, they should already be washed and ready to use. I sort my scraps according to color, then store them in clear plastic bags.

Thread

Six-Strand Embroidery Floss

Two strands of six-strand embroidery floss is most commonly used for buttonhole stitch appliqué. You can use one color of floss throughout the piece, or vary the colors for each appliqué motif. If you vary the colors, pick floss colors that enhance or accent the appliqué fabrics. I like using threads that are a little brighter or richer in color than the fabrics, so they outline the appliqué. It is fun stitching a purple deer in red thread! Look at the different projects in the book to see how I use contrasting threads.

Perle Cotton

Perle cotton is a twisted cotton thread. You only use one strand of perle cotton, and the strands do not need separating before stitching. DMC™ size 8 is the most appropriate size for buttonhole stitch appliqué. Perle cotton is an especially nice thread to use for stitching on wool projects.

Paper-Backed Adhesive

Paper-backed adhesive is a thin piece of fusible paper that has a web or dotted grid of adhesive on one side. The adhesive side is easily identified by its rough texture. The fusible paper is placed on the fabric with the adhesive facing the fabric. The adhesive sticks to the fabric when you apply heat to the paper backing. It is important to find a paper-backed adhesive that is "sewable." A light-weight adhesive is the easiest to stitch. Some adhesives are too heavy or too thick to get a needle through them. To avoid this problem, you should read the label carefully when you purchase an adhesive. You may want to buy ⅛ yard each of several types and experiment to find a brand you like. After purchase, always keep it stored in a roll with a rubber band around it. If it is folded, the adhesive web might pull away from the paper backing at the fold lines.

Needles

Sizes 6–8 embroidery or sharps needles work well for buttonhole stitch appliqué. When choosing a needle, keep two things in mind: the eye of the needle needs to be large enough for two strands of floss or one strand of perle cotton, and the needle tip needs to be sharp.

Scissors

Use paper scissors for cutting the paper-backed adhesive and paper patterns. Use good fabric scissors with sharp tips for cutting the appliqué motifs from the fabric.

Buttons, Ribbons, and Trimmings

Add interest to the overall design with all sizes and shapes of buttons, ribbons, and trimmings. Use buttons for the centers of flowers, or sprinkle them around motifs with a sewing theme (page 38) as decoration. Double the thread before stitching the buttons onto the fabric. Stitch each button separately. Work the thread through the button's holes twice, then knot the tails on the fabric back. This way, if one button comes loose, you won't lose the whole button cluster. Choose ribbons and trimmings that keep the style of the project in mind. Trimmings can be an assortment of laces, or other memorabilia. Ribbons can also be folded into bows, or used as accents around appliqué motifs. It is almost impossible to find the exact color of ribbon to match a fabric, so if your ribbons have a mood in common with the appliqué fabrics they will look fine.

Batting

Thinner, lightweight batting works well in banner quilts. Thinner batting allows the banner to lay flat against the wall. I prefer quilts to lie flat and not curl around the edges. Choose batts that have a minimum loft (the thickness of the batting) of 3 ounces.

Planning Colors

As you plan the colors, think about the theme you want to project. There are a variety of themes in this book, and you'll get many ideas as you look through the projects. The pink and green quilt, *Baskets and Fans* (page 72), has soft pastels. These colors project a romantic mood, making the quilt suitable for use in a woman's room or used as a baby's quilt. This quilt could also decorate a room furnished in white wicker. The *Pine Meadow* quilt (page 12) is a portrait of my home and yard. I live in the country and most every day I see the fish swimming in our pond, the snow-capped mountains, and the tall pine trees. Deer visit our yard and eat my flowers. Two of my favorite quilt blocks, Log Cabin and Sawtooth Star, I've added as appliqués. The colors and fabrics I used for this quilt are rich and bright.

All these elements combined together convey a folk-art mood. By following the format I've devised, you could easily make this your neighborhood with your own color scheme. I could see this quilt done in "early morning" pastels for a garden theme, or vibrant darks and lights for a "bright city night" quilt.

As I worked on the book, I found myself trying different styles of quilts. Once you have decided on the theme, select fabrics that have a mood in common. I like to think of all the possibilities as I choose fabrics, then eliminate ones that don't work. It seems easier to eliminate fabrics than to try find that "one more" piece of fabric you need. Think in terms of background verses appliqué fabrics. There needs to be enough contrast between the two elements for the appliqué motifs to show on the finished project. If the background is mellow, then the appliqués can be brighter and more intense. If the background is darker, then the fabrics need to be a lighter or medium color. Contrast is important in planning the appliqué and the background fabrics. You need to have contrast between the background fabric and the motifs in order to see the design. The contrast is emphasized by the sparkle: a small amount of brighter, more intense fabric that makes the other fabrics all work together. *Blackberry Pie* on page 30 uses a small amount of gold to accent the other fabrics. The deeper gold color creates direction and helps move the eye around the quilt; it also makes the other motifs show up better in the design. When I was choosing the fabrics for *Angelic Christmas* banner on page 80, the red, blue, and green fabrics were all the same value. Value is the difference in lightness or darkness of a color. When the colors were viewed from a distance, they looked dull

together. I put a small amount of hot pink fabric under the red heart and the design became vibrant. I repeated the same technique with a lime-green fabric under the green, then used a light gold for the angel wings. I call this technique the "echo rule." The key is to use a small amount of a more intense color, then position it under the color it complements, thus echoing the effect.

There are a variety of print fabrics in the projects. When selecting print fabrics, look at the scale in the print. The scale is the size of the design in a print. You want the scale of the print to work with the size of the appliqué motif. When choosing prints and plaids, you will find medium and smaller prints work better with appliqué motifs since the prints show some movement, but still read as subtle texture from a distance. Match the appliqué motifs with the texture of the prints; some print textures can mimic the tiles on a roof, leaves on a tree, or even scales on a fish. Remember, you don't have to cut with the grain for appliqué motifs. You can cut the shape at an angle to create a whimsical look. A larger print, however, will overpower a smaller appliqué motif. Larger prints are better suited in the borders because they often serve as a frame for the quilt and unify the fabrics. If you think about it, you can change the border design with a larger print

fabric just by varying the cut of the print. Changing the style of fabric from print to plaid to solid also creates interest in the design. I hope these new ideas will have you looking at fabrics in a new way.

Making Patterns

The patterns can be traced directly out of the book and onto the paper-backed adhesive. Or you may want to photocopy them, then cut them out. If the shapes are cut first, a one way design like the fish can be turned to face right or left. Designs such as the fish or blackbird motifs are one-way designs. You trace them onto the adhesive in the opposite direction that you want to see the finished design. When they are fused to the fabric, they reverse themselves. If you need several of one motif, stack the paper, pin the layers together in the center, then cut all the layers at once.

When I am creating a design, I like to have all of the motifs already cut and spread out in front of me, so I have lots of options. You might want to enlarge and reduce some of the designs on a copy machine so you can choose from several different sizes. Make notes on the motifs as to the increase or decrease from the original (example: 20% increase). Store the paper patterns in a plastic bag or a box labeled with the project name.

Fuse the Appliqués

1 With a pencil, trace the appliqué motif onto the paper side of the adhesive. Use a ruler when tracing straight lines to keep them level.

2 Cut around the motif with a paper scissors. Leave a small amount of paper beyond the pencil line, so you can see the outline of the shape.

3 Place the adhesive side (rough side) of the fusible paper onto the wrong side of the fabric. Following the manufacturer's instructions for the paper-backed adhesive, fuse the adhesive to the fabric. Do Not Overheat! If you do, the adhesive may melt through the fabric.

4 Use small, sharp fabric scissors to cut the traced motif on the pencil line. Peel off the paper backing. If the paper-backing is difficult to remove, use a pin to loosen it first.

5 Position the appliqué motif on the background fabric. When you are satisfied with the placement of the motif, fuse it to the fabric following the manufacturer's instructions. If you have to fuse several layers together, lightly press each motif in place as you build the layers. When all the layers are in place, fuse them together following the manufacturer's instructions.

I like using a flat, hard surface to fuse fabrics, because fusing is easier if there is no fabric hanging over an edge. When there is a lot of fusing to do, use a tabletop with a towel over it. Do not use your good dining room table, because the heat of the iron will make the towel stick to the table's top.

Buttonhole Stitching

This stitch actually has two names: buttonhole and blanket. If the stitches are worked close together, it is called a buttonhole stitch. When the stitches are further apart, it is a blanket stitch. Because the stitch is commonly called buttonhole stitch, I use this name throughout the book, regardless of how close the stitches are placed.

The buttonhole stitch is a decorative embroidery stitch that holds the appliqué motif in place after the shape is fused to the background fabric. The stitch lies along the border of the motif and hides the fabrics raw edges. Work the stitch from left to right. I hold the fabric so I can work the stitch with the needle tip pointed away from me.

Start by cutting an 18" length of thread from the skein of embroidery floss (or use one strand of perle cotton). Separate two strands from the cut floss, then place the two strands back together and knot an end. Thread the opposite end through the needle. You are now ready to start stitching. Bring the needle tip up from the back of the fabric so it appears at the raw edge of the appliqué motif. Pull the thread through to the knot. About ⅛" from the appliqué edge, insert the needle into the fabric and emerge parallel to the appliqué edge, bringing the needle tip over the working thread. Pull the stitch into place until the thread along the edge is secure and slightly taut.

Hold the working thread with your left thumb and take another stitch. Repeat the process to continue stitching.

Each buttonhole stitch needs to have the same amount of tension, or they will look loopy. By holding the working thread with your thumb while you work the next stitch, the stitch tension is kept constant.

Sizing the Stitch

To keep the stitching proportional to the motif, vary the size of the stitch with the size of the appliqué. On a tiny star, the stitch might be ⅛" in length, whereas on a large tree, it might be ¼" in length. A smaller, more intricate motif requires a shorter stitch length that is spaced closer together. Try to keep a consistent distance when spacing the stitches apart. You want the stitches to look like they flow evenly. But, this is a folk-art style of stitching, so if there is some variation it will look just fine.

Stitching Points and Corners

As you approach a narrow point, like the tip of the fir trees in the *Pine Meadow* quilt (page 12), emerge with the needle tip at the top edge of the point, then insert the needle back into the fabric, as if you are ending the stitch. This forms a little catch stitch and it will hold the thread in place at the point's edge. Bring the needle up again a couple of fabric threads over (shown with the dot in the illustration), and start stitching to form the new buttonhole stitch.

Stitching Curves

As you approach a curve, plan your stitches so that they are equal distance apart and flow evenly around the edges. The "legs" of the stitches will be closer together inside the curve, and will fan at the curve's edges.

A machine buttonhole stitch can be used for appliqué motifs with straight edges, but it doesn't work well on curves. Read your machine manual to find the correct settings. Use a heavier thread, such as buttonhole thread, and a larger needle in your machine. Practice the stitch before trying it on your quilt top.

Stitching the Quilt Top Together

Each of the quilt schematics are labeled with Blocks A, B, C, etc. This sequence of letters is the piecing sequence. Block A needs to be stitched to Block B before you can add Block C. Use ¼" seam allowance.

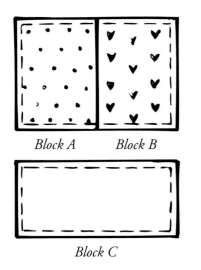

Block A   *Block B*

Block C

When pressing the blocks together, press the seam toward the darker fabric. Wherever several seams meet, press them so they lay in opposite directions, regardless if the seam won't be pressed toward the darker fabric. In some cases, such as the Pine Meadow quilt on page 12, the appliqué edges in the mountain landscape block are included in the seam, but the Log Cabin and Sawtooth Star blocks are not.

When you are ready to add the borders, refer to the schematic to see if the sides, or the top and bottom borders are added first. To add a border strip, lay the strip on the front of the quilt top, with right sides facing. Sew with a ¼" seam allowance, then press the seam allowances toward the border strips. Repeat the sequence for the remaining strips. The design of the quilt determines the border construction sequence.

Finishing the Quilts

Most of the quilting is done by outlining the appliqué motifs and stitching within the seams. Because the quilt designs emphasize the appliqués, too intricate quilting designs take away from look of the quilt. The quilts having more background fabric have more decorative stitching showing. *Blackberry Pie* on page 30 has diagonal lines quilted in the background fabric. I like to use echo quilting (outlining or repeating the motif) to enhance the theme of the quilt. There are numerous stencils available that can be used to trace designs on the fabric. Use a washable pencil if you are marking the quilting lines, but try it on a scrap of fabric

first. Use a gridded ruler to mark straight lines. Re-usable quarter-inch masking tape is available to mark straight lines when the quilt layers are already together.

1 Prepare the quilt backing by piecing any seams needed to create the quilt size. I have planned the batting and backing to be at least one inch larger than the finished size all around. Press the backing so the seams lay flat. Place the backing, with the wrong side facing up, on a large table. Use masking tape to tape each corner to the table. Pull the backing fabric taut. Add tape to the middle of each side and work toward the corners. Tape at even intervals to keep the fabric taut as you work.

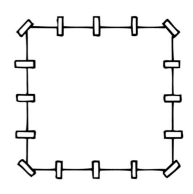

2 To layer the quilt, place the batting over the backing fabric. Smoothing away any bumps. Add the quilt top, with the right side facing up and centered over the batting and backing.

3 Basting may be done with safety pins or thread. If you plan to machine quilt, use pins to baste the layers together. Start at the

center and place the pins about 5" apart. For hand quilting, either the thread or pin basting methods will work. To baste with thread, work with a threaded embroidery needle and start at the quilt center. Using the arrows in the illustration as a guide, baste to the quilt corners.

4 Machine or hand quilt the projects using your preferred method. Use a walking foot for machine quilting to keep the layers feeding evenly through the machine. Echo quilt around the motifs and "stitch in the ditch" (as close to the seam as possible) around the blocks and borders. Specific quilting instructions may appear within a quilt's individual project instructions. Hand quilt with a short, sharp needle called a "betweens." Use a size 8-12 needle, depending on the thickness of the batting. Use a single thread about 18" long and knotted at one end. Remove any basting when you've finished quilting.

5 Before adding the binding, check the individual project instructions to find the length of the edges. Add one side binding first. Sew the side binding strip to the edge of the quilt, with right sides together and using ¼" seam allowance. Trim any excess batting or backing fabric. Press the raw edge of the binding strip under ¼". Fold the binding to the back of the quilt and align the folded edge with the seam line. Pin every few inches.

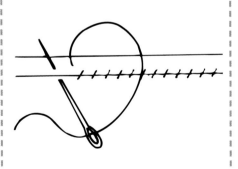

Slipstitch the binding to the back of the quilt.

6 Repeat the process to add the remaining side, top, and bottom binding strips. At the corners, fold under the raw edges of the top and bottom binding strips so they are even with the side edges of the quilt, and slipstitch.

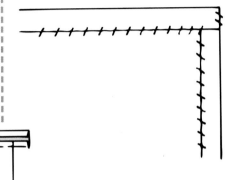

Pine Meadow Quilt

Pine Meadow is a sampler quilt full of whimsical Northwest motifs: a cabin amid the alpine trees, colorful swimming trout, lively deer, snow-topped mountains high, and stars filling the evening skies. The Sawtooth Star and Log Cabin blocks are appliquéd instead of pieced. To individualize your sampler quilt, move the blocks or appliqué motifs around or add some new motifs of your own. The finished size is 38½"x 39½".

Supplies Needed

You may use the colors in the original project, but feel free to substitute with your own choices.

- Block A: ½ yard
- Block B: ¼ yard
- Blocks C, D, E, F, and G: five 4½" squares of coordinating colors
- Block H: ¼ yard
- Block I: ¼ yard
- Block J: ⅛ yard
- Blocks K: ¼ yard
- Blocks L: ½ yard
- Appliqué motifs: a variety of light, dark, medium, and bright colors totaling 2 yards
- Backing: 1¼ yards
- Batting: 41" x 42"
- Binding: ¼ yard
- Paper-backed adhesive 3 yards
- Embroidery floss: coordinating colors totaling 5 skeins

Cutting Guide

- Block A: cut a 16½" square
- Block B: cut a 4½" x 16½" rectangle
- Blocks C, D, E, F, and G are pre-cut.
- Block H: cut a 6½"x 20½" rectangle
- Block I: cut an 8½" x 26½" rectangle
- Block J: cut a 3½" x 28½" rectangle
- Blocks K (First border): cut four strips 1½" x 42". From the strips, cut two strips 29½" for the sides and two strips 30½" for the top and bottom.

- Blocks L (Second border): cut four strips 4½" x 42". From the strips, cut two strips 39½" for the sides and cut two strips 30½" for top and bottom.
- Backing: cut one piece 41" x 42"
- Binding: cut four strips 1¾" x 42". From the strips, cut two strips 39½" for the sides and two strips 39" for the top and bottom.

Tracing Guide

Trace the following appliqué shapes onto the paper-backed adhesive:

- Block A: one cabin, six alpine trees (choose any combination), five small stars, one moon, one dog

- Block B: four each of Log Cabin patterns 1-9
- Blocks C, D, E, F, and G: five each of Sawtooth Star patterns 1-2
- Block H: one each of mountain landscape patterns 5-12 and sunset patterns 1-4
- Block I: four assorted alpine trees, two deer, six assorted stars
- Block J: four small trout
- Blocks L (border total): 19 assorted alpine trees, eight stars, five Sawtooth Stars, one deer, one small trout, two moons

Pine Meadow Quilt

Sewing Instructions

Use ¼" seam allowance.

1 Follow the instructions on pages 8-9 to fuse all the motifs onto the appliqué fabrics, then cut the shapes. Fuse the motifs onto the background fabric for each block. For Block B, press the background fabric into four equal squares. Keep a ¼" seam allowance remaining around the edge of the block. Arrange the Log Cabin pieces for each square onto the background fabric, starting with pattern 1 in the center. Using tweezers to help arrange the pieces, leave a small space between each piece for the buttonhole stitching. Lightly press each piece, and after all the pieces are in place for each square, fuse the pieces following the manufacturer's instructions.

For the Blocks C, D, E, F, and G, center and fuse each Sawtooth Star piece onto the background fabric. Keep a ¼"

Block B

seam allowance remaining around the edge of each block.

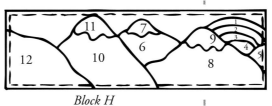

Blocks C, D, E, F, G

For Block H, fuse the landscape pieces following the numbered sequence onto the background fabric. The dashed lines on the pattern pieces indicate where overlapping takes place. The edges of the appliqué pieces will overlap into the ¼" seam allowance around the edge of the block. I have already turned the patterns over so your mountains will look just like mine when you fuse them onto the block. (Remember, the one way designs reverse themselves.)

Block H

Buttonhole stitch around all the motifs following the instructions on page 9. The deer on the upper right-hand corner of the second border cannot be fused in place until the border is stitched onto the quilt.

2 Stitch the blocks together. The sequence of block construction follows the letters given to the blocks. Stitch Block A to B, then join C through G and add to Block A/B. Next add Block H, then I, then J.

3 When you get to the first border (Blocks K), add the side strips first, then the top and bottom strips following the instructions on page 10. For the second border (Blocks L), add the top and bottom strips first, then the side strips. Fuse the last deer to the upper right-hand corner and buttonhole stitch the motif in place.

4 Machine quilt in the ditch for all the seams, then echo quilt around the major appliqué shapes. If you feel more background quilting is needed, try cross-hatch quilting. Cross-hatching is quilting parallel lines running in two directions, forming either a grid of squares or diamonds depending on the slant of the crossed quilting lines.

Finish the quilt according to the instructions on page 10.

Wildlife Pillows

The wildlife pillows follow the same theme as the *Pine Meadow* quilt in design and mood of fabrics. The pillow's background formats are the same, only the appliqué motifs are different. This is a flange-style pillow where the inner pocket holds the pillow form, and the outer, flat edge acts as a border. The *Deer Lodge* pillow sports large rickrack along the seam separating the pillow design and the flange border. The finished size is 20" x 20".

Supplies Needed

The fabric listing is for one pillow. You may use the colors in the original project, but feel free to substitute with your own choices.

- Block A: ¼ yard
- Block B: ⅓ yard
- Blocks C and D, and Back: ¾ yard

- Appliqué motifs: For the *Trout Lake* pillow: 5" x 11" rectangle for one large trout, 7" x 8" rectangles of coordinating colors for three alpine trees, plus scraps for trunks and for one moon. For *Deer Lodge* pillow: 5"x 7" rectangles of coordinating colors for two alpine trees, 8" x 9"

rectangle for one large deer, scrap fabric for one moon

- 16" square pillow form
- Paper-backed adhesive: 1 yard
- Embroidery floss: a variety of colors totaling 1 skein
- Optional: 2 yards of large rickrack for *Deer Lodge* pillow

Cutting Guide

- Block A: cut a 6½" x 16½" rectangle
- Block B: cut a 10½" x 16½" rectangle
- Block C: cut two 2½" x 16½" rectangles
- Block D: cut two 2½" x 20½" rectangles
- Back: cut two 12½" x 20½" pieces
- Rickrack: cut four 16½" lengths for the *Deer Lodge* pillow

Tracing Guide

Trace the following appliqué shapes onto the paper-backed adhesive:

- For the *Trout Lake* pillow: one large trout, three alpine trees, one moon
- For the *Deer Lodge* pillow: one large deer, two alpine trees, one moon

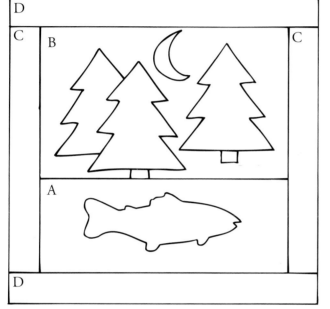

Trout Lake

Deer Lodge

Wildlife Pillows

Sewing Instructions

Use ¼" seam allowance.

1 Stitch Block A to Block B. For the *Deer Lodge* pillow, mark the ¼" seam line around the edges for Block A/B. Center the width of the rickrack pieces over the marked seam line. Overlap the rickrack at the corners. Following the border instructions on page 10, add Block C to the sides first, then Block D to the top and bottom. The rickrack will be caught in the seam when the borders are attached. Follow the instructions on pages 8-9 to fuse the motifs onto the appliqué fabrics, then cut the shapes. Fuse the motifs onto the background fabric. Buttonhole stitch around all the motifs following the instructions on page 9.

2 Machine hem one 20½" edge of each back piece. Place one back piece over the pillow front, with right sides facing and the hemmed edge to the center. Repeat for the other back piece, overlapping the hemmed edges at the pillow center. Pin the raw edges together.

3 Stitch the pillow front and back together (right sides are facing). Trim the corners. Turn to the right side and press. Machine stitch in the ditch at the inner border seams, creating a flange border. Slip in the pillow form.

Fisherman's Friend Sport Shirt

This is a perfect gift for the fisherman in your family. I found a khaki colored shirt and added the medium trout appliqué above the pocket. Green floss highlights the colorful motif fabric, but I used a darker floss color and added extra stitching around the collar and pocket.

Supplies Needed

- Purchased shirt
- Appliqué motif: scrap fabric for medium trout
- Paper-backed adhesive: ⅛ yard
- Embroidery floss: a variety of colors totaling 1 skein

Tracing Guide

Trace the medium trout appliqué shape onto the paper-backed adhesive.

Sewing Instructions

1 Follow the instructions on pages 8-9 to fuse the trout motif onto the appliqué fabric, then cut the shape. Fuse the trout onto the shirt and buttonhole stitch, following the instructions on page 9. Decorate the collar and pocket with buttonhole stitching.

Spring Jubilee Jacket

Colorful appliqués in cotton and wool adorn this purchased jacket. The jacket already had black, machine-buttonhole stitching around the edges. With the jacket color being so dark, the brighter, richer colors in the appliqués showed up better. As you start adding appliqués onto the jacket, ideas will come to you as you stitch. I started with the bird, then thought about adding the tulips coming out of the other pocket. Next, I felt like the bird needed a birdhouse. (Of course, he is too big to get into that house!) This whimsical style adds more fun to the projects. Hearts are scattered around the collar along with a variety of wood and metal buttons. Taking the heart appliqué and cutting it in half added more interest. The buttons are clustered along the edge of the house, creating an interesting roof line. You'll notice I used a variety of floss colors to stitch the appliqués in place.

Supplies Needed

You may use the colors in the original project, but feel free to substitute with your own choices.

- Purchased jacket
- Appliqué motifs: scrap fabrics of cotton and wool (if you can find it)
- Paper-backed adhesive: 1 yard
- Buttons: thirty ½" to ⅞"-wide wood and metal buttons
- Bird's eye: one ¼"-wide black bead or button
- Embroidery floss: a variety of colors totaling 2 skeins

Tracing Guide

Trace the following appliqué shapes onto the paper-backed adhesive:

- one bird, six medium split hearts, one medium heart, one large split heart, three triangles, three circles, one birdhouse, three tulips, three stems, six leaves, three small stars

Sewing Instructions

1. Follow the instructions on pages 8-9 to fuse the motifs onto the appliqué fabrics, then cut the shapes. Fuse the motifs onto the jacket using the photo as a guide. Buttonhole stitch around all the motifs following the instructions on page 9. Using the photo as a guide and referring to the instructions on page 7, stitch the buttons onto the jacket.

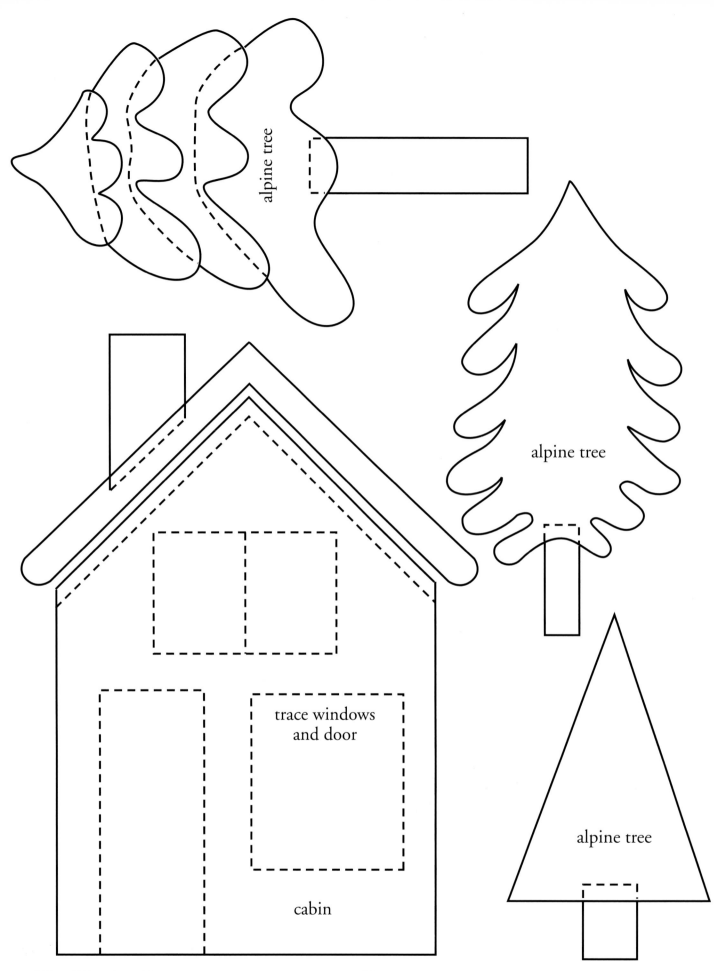

alpine tree

alpine tree

trace windows
and door

cabin

alpine tree

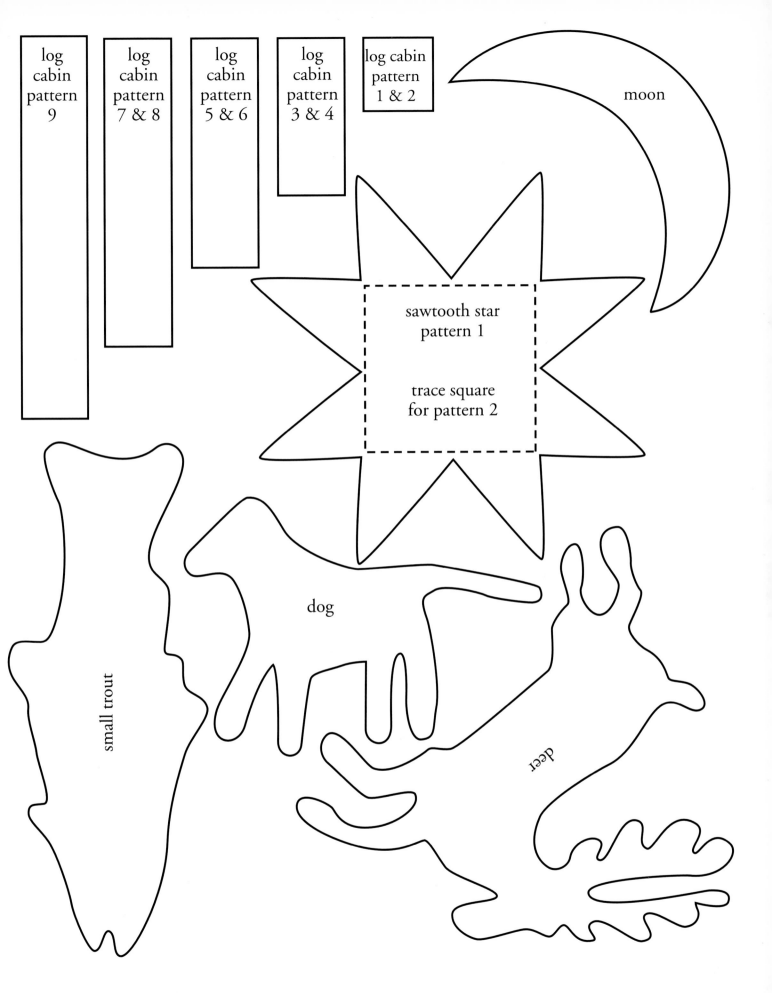

log cabin pattern 9

log cabin pattern 7 & 8

log cabin pattern 5 & 6

log cabin pattern 3 & 4

log cabin pattern 1 & 2

moon

sawtooth star pattern 1

trace square for pattern 2

small trout

dog

deer

Pine Meadow Patterns

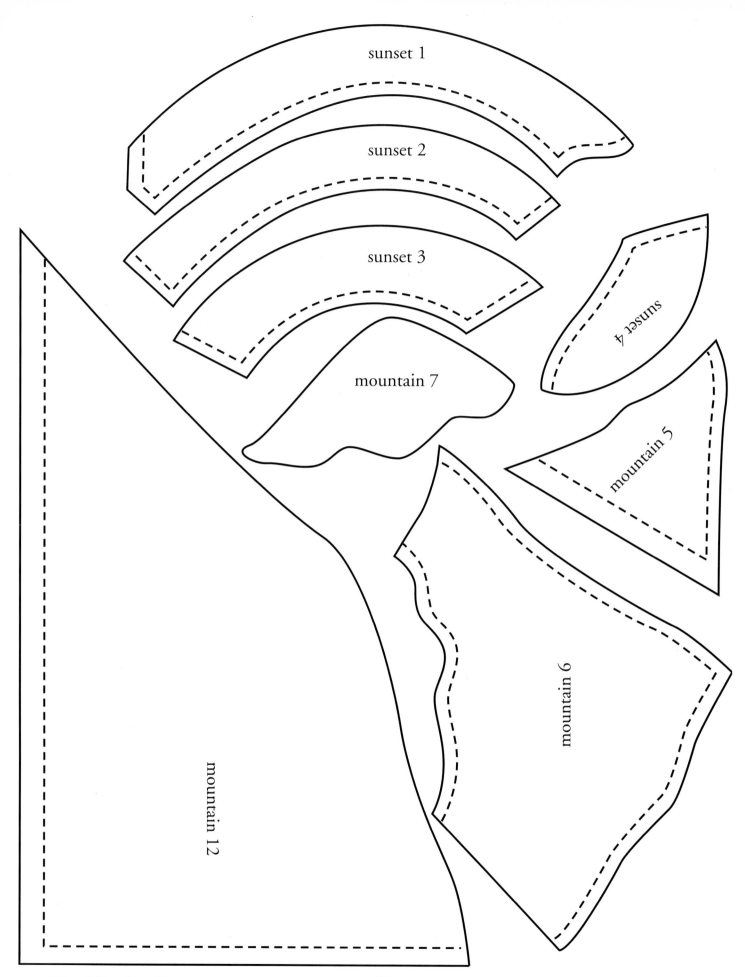

sunset 1

sunset 2

sunset 3

sunset 4

mountain 7

mountain 5

mountain 6

mountain 12

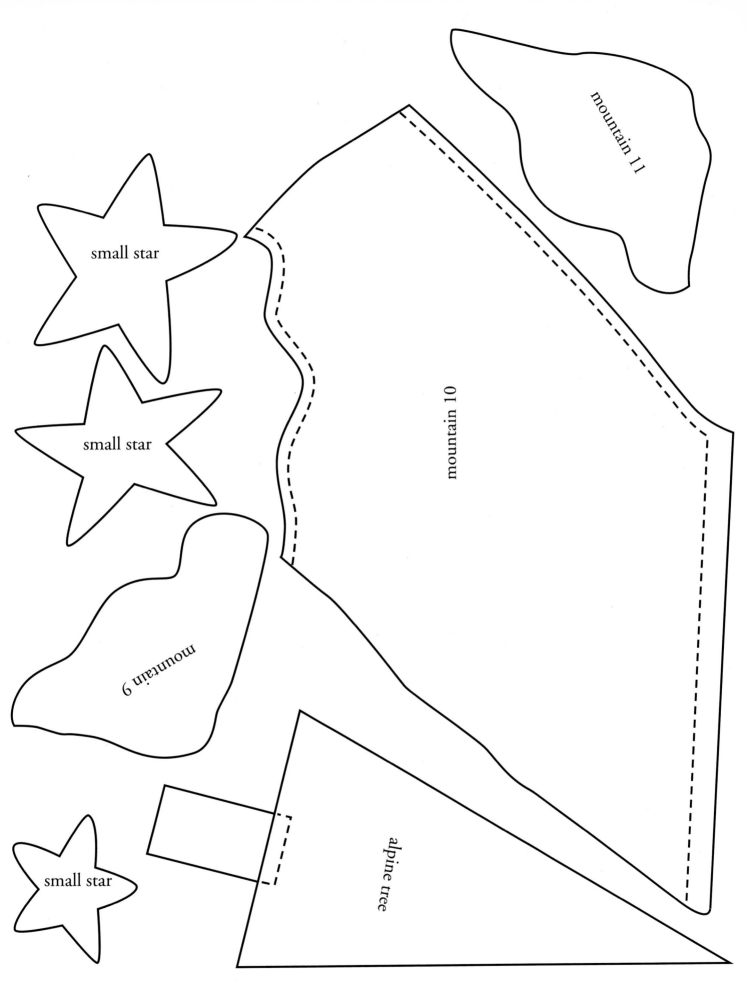

mountain 11

small star

small star

mountain 10

mountain 9

small star

alpine tree

Pine Meadow Patterns

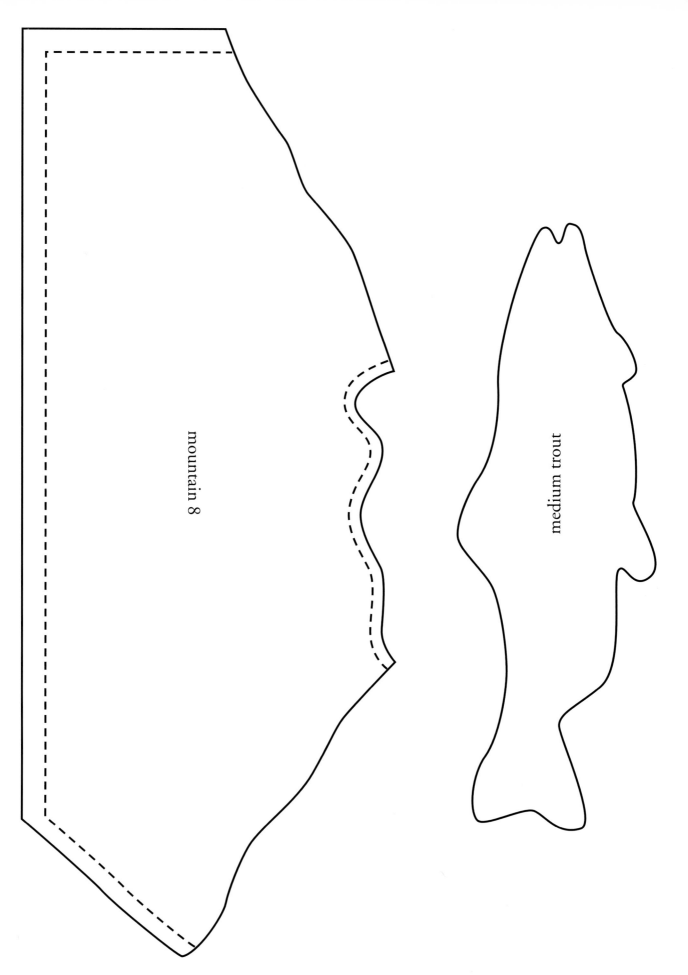

mountain 8

medium trout

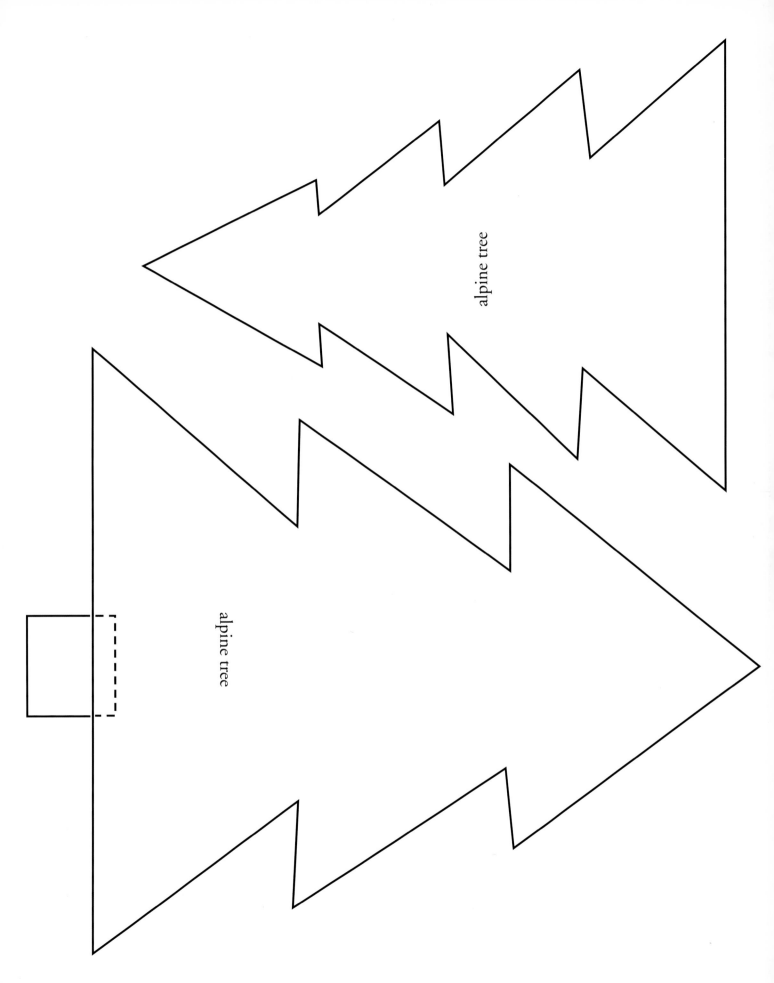

alpine tree

alpine tree

Pine Meadow Patterns

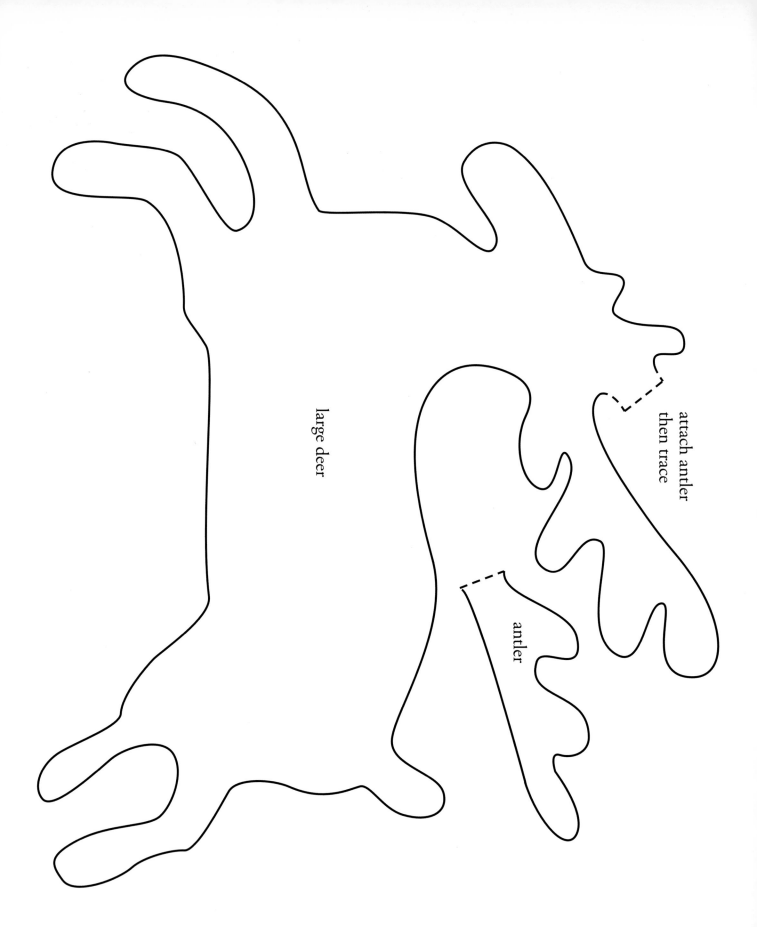

large deer

attach antler
then trace

antler

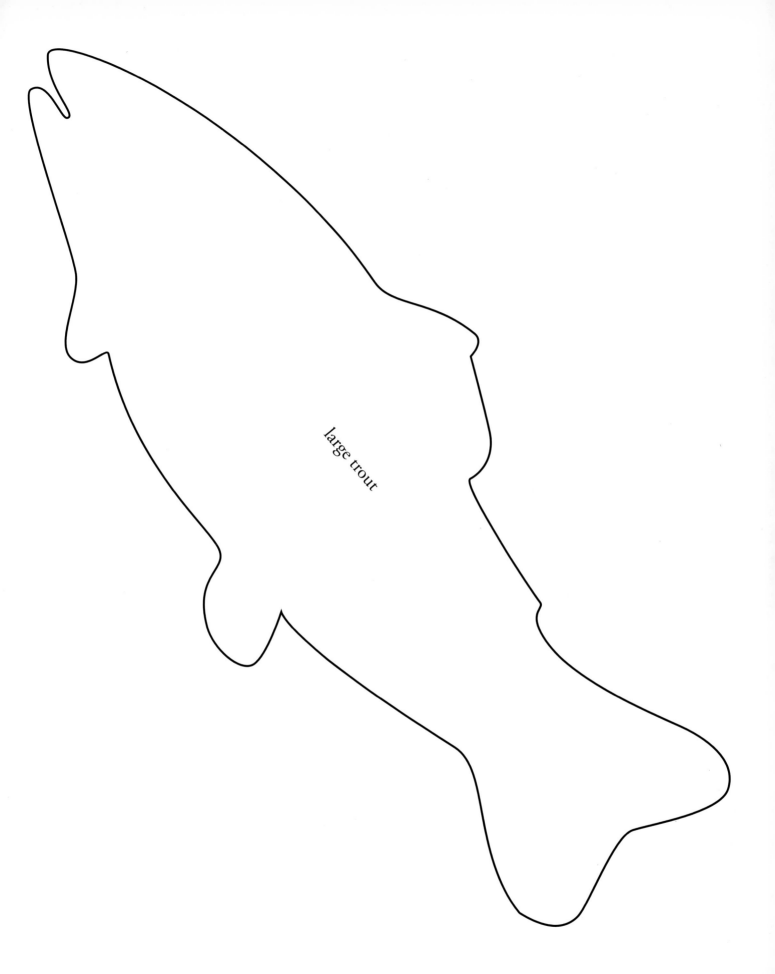

large trout

Pine Meadow Patterns

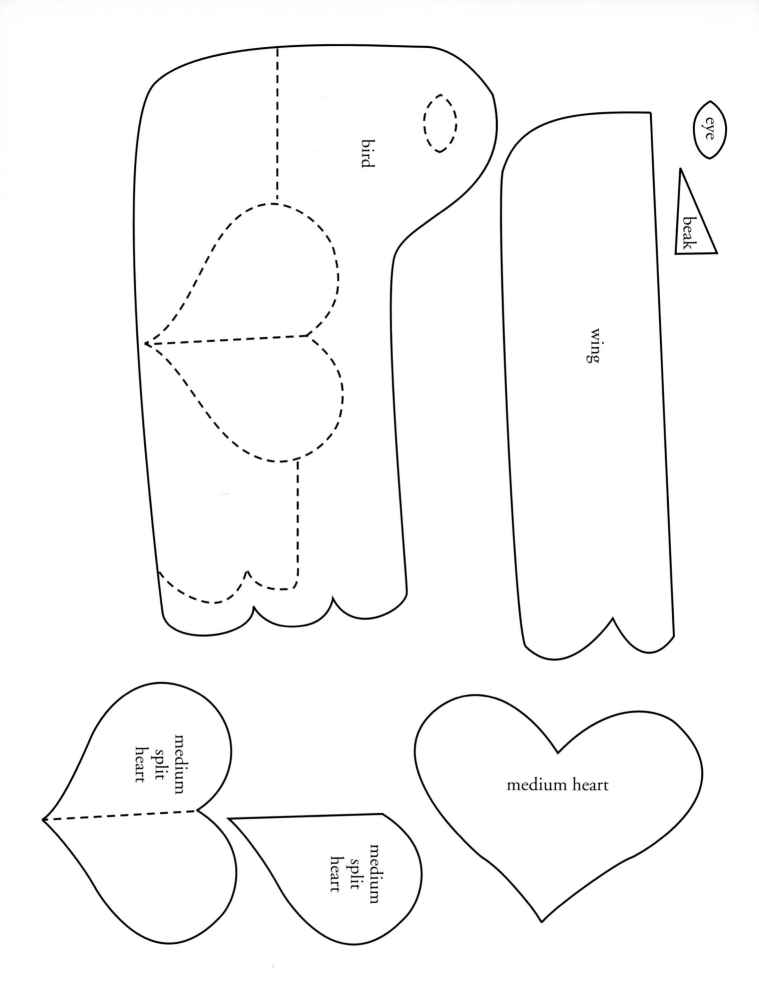

bird

eye

beak

wing

medium split heart

medium split heart

medium heart

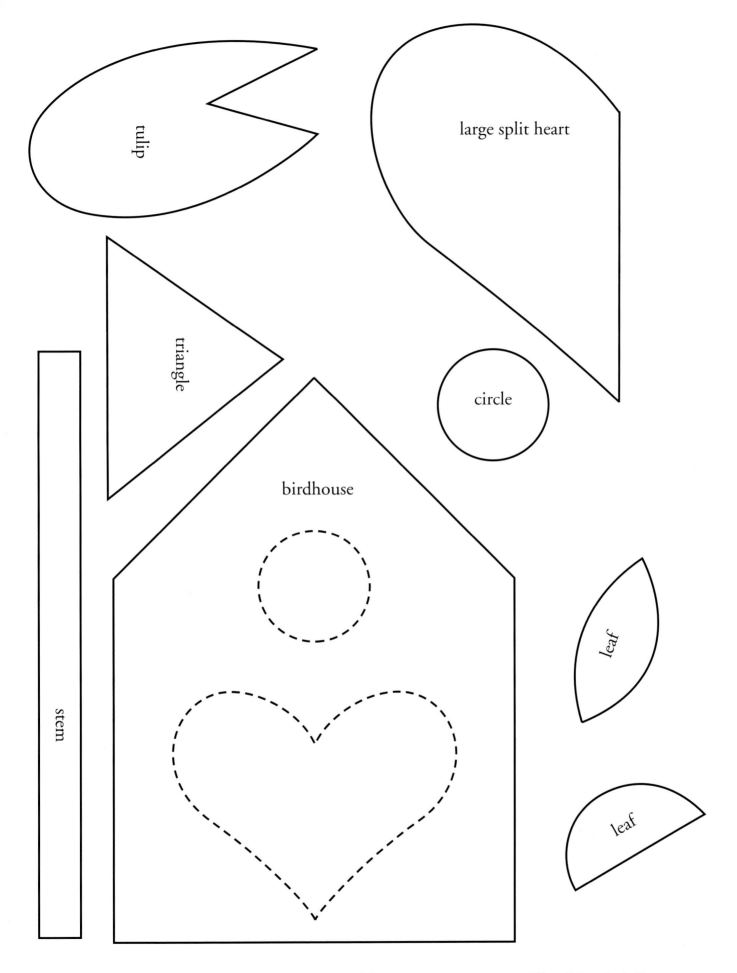

tulip

large split heart

triangle

circle

stem

birdhouse

leaf

leaf

Blackberry Pie Quilt

This is the first quilt I designed for the book. The colors remind me of a blackberry pie poster I saw years ago. The appliqué colors vibrate from the black background, and electric blue fabric behind the yellow vines pulls the eye around the design. Andrea Balosky, a quilting friend of mine, hand quilted the background fabric using red thread; this extra touch adds much warmth to the spirited design. The finished size is 28" x 28".

Supplies Needed

You may use the colors in the original project, but feel free to substitute with your own choices.

- Blocks A, C, D, E, and binding: 1 yard
- Blocks B: ⅓ yard
- Border inset: ¼ yard
- Appliqué motifs: ¼ yard for vines, ⅛ yard for birds, ¼ yard of coordinating colors for center heart, ¼ yard of coordinating colors for flowers and leaves, ⅛ yard of coordinating colors for baskets and fans
- Backing: 1 yard
- Batting: 30" x 30"
- Paper-backed adhesive: 2 yards
- Embroidery floss: a variety of colors totaling 2 skeins

Cutting Guide

- Block A: cut a 12" square
- Blocks B: cut a strip 5" x 42" and one 5" x 12". Cut three 12" strips from the longer strip.
- Blocks C: cut a strip 5" x 20". Cut the strip into four 5" squares.
- Blocks D: cut two strips 4" x 42". Cut each strip into two 21" strips.
- Blocks E: cut a strip 4" x 16". Cut the strip into four 4" squares.
- Border inset: cut two strips 1" x 42", and one strip 1" x 32". From the strips, cut two 21" strips, two 28" strips, and four 4" strips.
- Binding: cut two strips 1¾" x 28" for the sides, and two strips 1¾" x 28½" for the top and bottom.
- Backing: cut a 30" square

Tracing Guide

Trace the following appliqué shapes onto the paper-backed adhesive:

- Block A: one each of center heart patterns 1-5, plus four of fan wedge pattern 6
- Blocks B (total): four vines and birds, 12 flower patterns 1-2, 16 leaves
- Block C: four each of basket patterns 1-3
- Blocks E: 16 of fan wedge pattern 6 (from center heart)

Blackberry Pie Quilt

Sewing Instructions

Use ¼" seam allowance.

1 Follow the instructions on pages 8-9 to fuse all the motifs onto the appliqué fabrics, then cut the shapes. Fuse the motifs onto the background fabric for each block. Start with pattern 1 and layer the heart (the dashed lines indicate where overlapping takes place). Keep a ¼" seam allowance remaining around the edge of each block. Buttonhole stitch around all the motifs following the instructions on page 9.

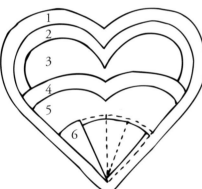

2 Stitch the blocks together, following the sequence of the letters given to the blocks. Stitch a Block B to the two sides of Block A (wait to add a Block B to the top and bottom of Block A). Stitch a Block C on both ends of the remaining Blocks B. Now add a Block B/C to the top and bottom of Block A/B.

3 Fold the border insets in half lengthwise and press. Matching raw edges, baste the 21"-long insets on the top and bottom of the quilt center. For the border, add a Block D to the top and bottom of the quilt center, following the instructions on page 10. After the blocks are sewn, the border inset will show ¼" of the folded fabric, forming a tiny accent border. Add the 28"-long insets to the sides of the quilt. Stitch the 4"-long insets to the ends of the remaining Blocks D. To complete the border, add a Block E to the ends of the remaining Blocks D, then add to the quilt sides.

4 Andrea outlined the heart area with accent quilting, then stitched double lines one inch apart for the background quilting. Finish the quilt according to the instructions on page 10.

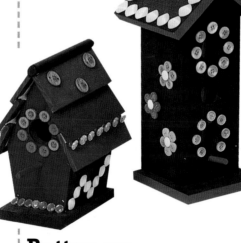

Button-up Birdhouses

These birdhouses were purchased unfinished from a craft store. I used acrylic paint, then glued buttons with a hot-glue gun. Arrange the buttons in flower shapes, outline the edges, or just scatter them within a design. I'm not sure if the birds in my neighborhood will inhabit them—but if they don't, these colorful houses make great decorations inside the house.

Supplies Needed

The listing is for one birdhouse.

- Unfinished purchased birdhouse
- Acrylic craft paints
- Small foam paint brushes (one for each color)
- Assorted buttons: mine came from bulk buttons I purchased by the cupful
- Hot glue gun, or small flat head nails and a hammer (for applying buttons

Instructions

1 Paint the birdhouse. The foam brushes can be rinsed out and used again. You may need to apply two coats of the darker colors.

Plan your own decorations, using the three examples as a guide. Attach the buttons using either a glue gun or small nails placed into the button's holes.

Hopping Bunnies Coat

I made this car coat from a commercial pattern (size 4), but you could easily decorate a purchased coat or denim jacket. This jacket is constructed of boiled wool. I embellished the edges with large rickrack and striped cotton binding.

Supplies Needed

You may use the appliqué colors in the original project, but feel free to substitute with your own choices.

- Purchased or constructed car coat
- Appliqué motifs: ¼ yard felt for bunnies, ⅛ yard for birds, ⅛ yard for flowers, ⅛ yard for leaves and hearts
- Large rickrack: 3 yards (optional for purchased garment)
- Binding: 3 yards (optional for purchased garment)
- Embroidery floss: a variety of colors totaling 2 skeins

Cutting Guide

- Binding: measure around the garment edges to determine the length of binding strips and rickrack needed. I cut the fabric strips 1¾" wide on the straight of grain.

Tracing Guide

Trace the following appliqué shapes onto the paper-backed adhesive:

- four bunnies (two facing right and two facing left), five birds, 15 flowers, 21 leaves, and three stacked hearts

Sewing Instructions

1 Follow the instructions on pages 8-9 to fuse the motifs onto the appliqué fabrics, then cut the shapes. Fuse the motifs onto the jacket using the photo as a guide. Buttonhole stitch around all the motifs following the instructions on page 9. Add the rickrack and binding to the edges if you have constructed a coat, using the binding instructions on page 11 as a guide.

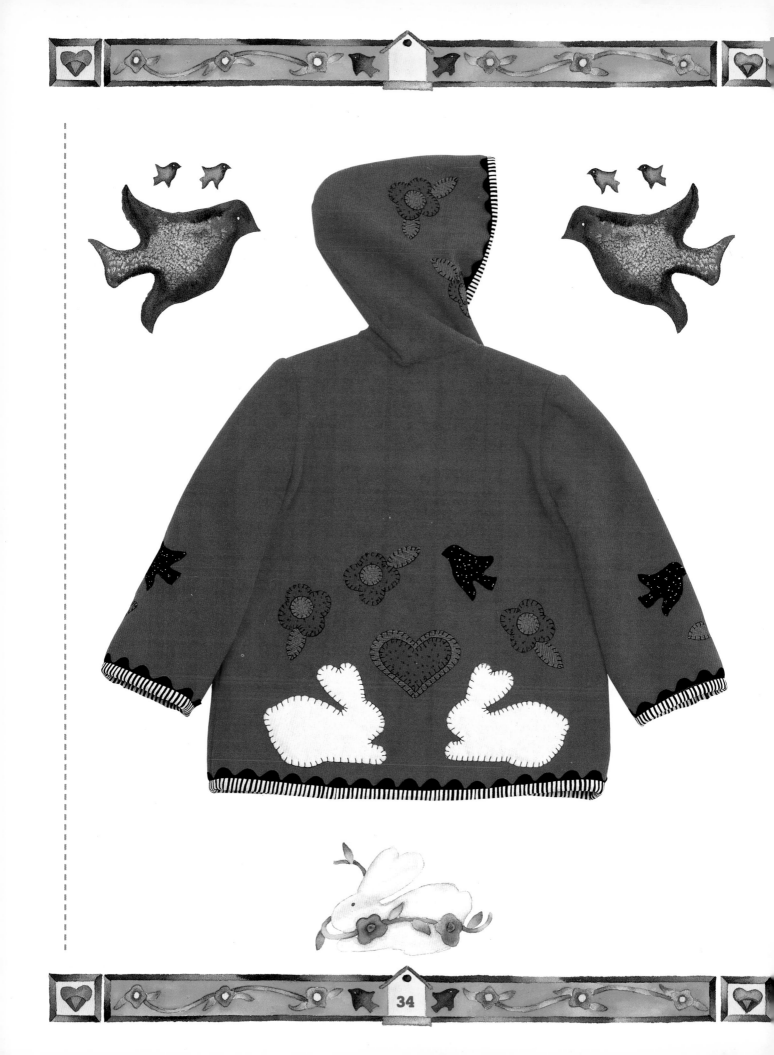

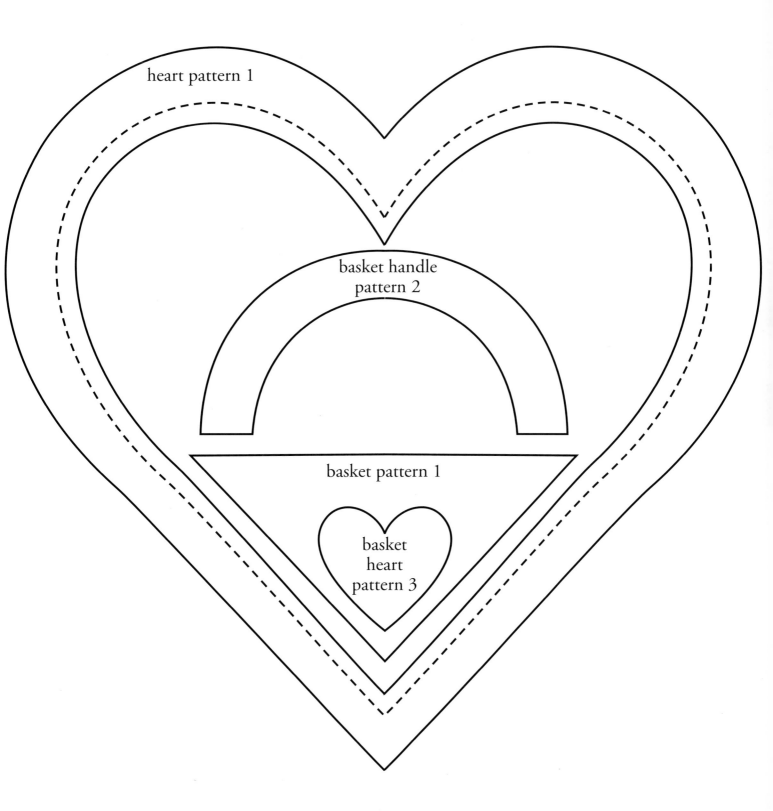

heart pattern 1

basket handle
pattern 2

basket pattern 1

basket
heart
pattern 3

Blackberry Pie Patterns

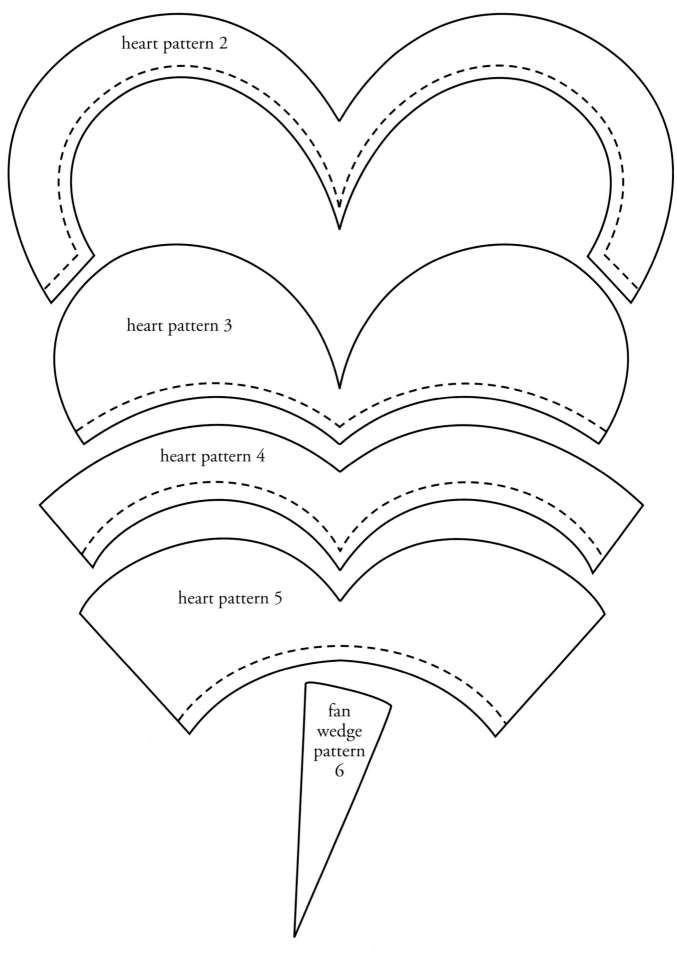

heart pattern 2

heart pattern 3

heart pattern 4

heart pattern 5

fan wedge pattern 6

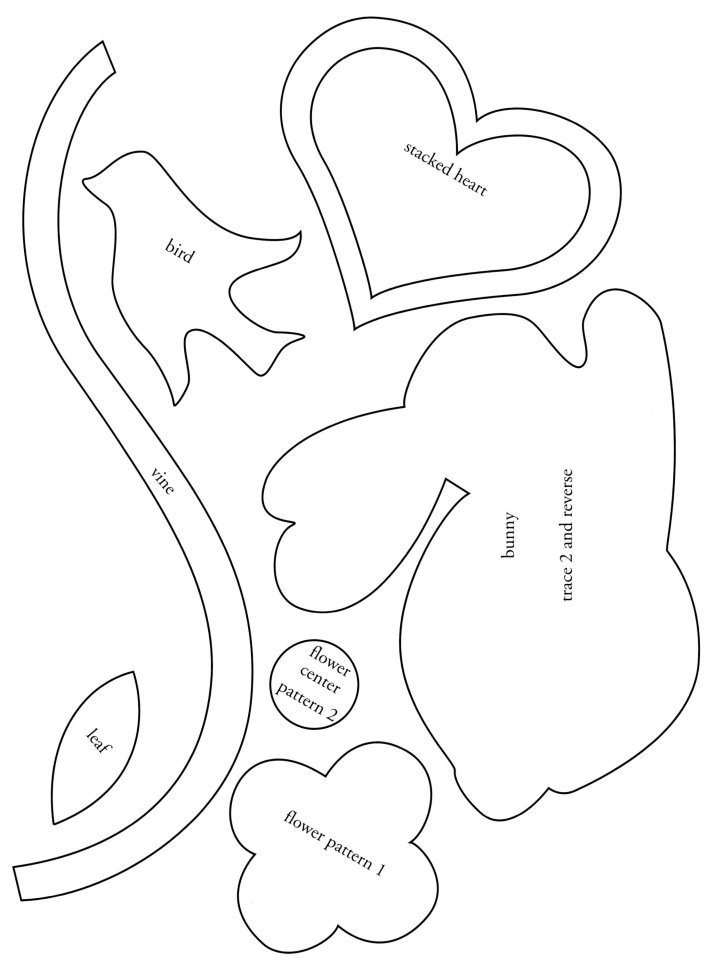

stacked heart

bird

vine

bunny

trace 2 and reverse

flower center pattern 2

leaf

flower pattern 1

37

Blackberry Pie Patterns

Sewing Essentials Caddy

I have always wanted to design a caddy for the wall above my sewing machine. A caddy should hold all the tools you use the most. This caddy has lined pockets for everything I can think of, plus I've added a stuffed pincushion. I used the colors from the printed background fabric as inspiration for choosing other colors in this design. The finished size is 29"x 26".

Supplies Needed

You may use the colors in the original project, but feel free to substitute with your own choices.

- Pockets B, C, D, E, and Blocks A and F: 1¼ yards
- Appliqué motifs: ⅛ yard each of five coordinating colors for the sewing motifs and ¼ yard for the sewing-machine motif
- Caddy front and backing: 1½ yards
- Buttons: sixty ½" to 1¼"-wide colored buttons
- Elastic: ⅔ yard of ⅞"-wide elastic for spool holder on Block F
- Polyester fiberfill: small wad for stuffing pincushion
- Ribbon: ⅓ yard of ⅞"-wide ribbon for loop hangers, 1 yard of Offray® tape measure ribbon for motif
- Monofilamet thread
- Batting: 29½" x 26½"
- Paper-backed adhesive: 1½ yards
- Embroidery floss: a variety of colors totaling 3 skeins

Cutting Guide

- Block A: cut two 12½" x 14½" rectangles
- Pockets B: cut four 5½" x 7" rectangles
- Pocket C: cut two 8½" x 12½" rectangles
- Pockets D: cut four 5" x 7" rectangles
- Pocket E: cut two using the pattern
- Block F: cut two 4" x 14½" rectangles
- Caddy front and backing: cut two 29½" x 26½" rectangles
- Pincushion: cut two using the pattern
- Ribbon: cut the ⅞"-wide ribbon into five 2" lengths

Tracing Guide

Trace the following appliqué shapes onto the paper-backed adhesive:

- Block A: sewing machine and small heart
- Pocket B: one scissors, large spool and needle
- Pocket C: large pincushion with heart and leaf, three small spools
- Pocket D: two small spools
- Pocket E: two small hearts

Sewing Essentials Caddy

Sewing Instructions

Use ¼" seam allowance.

1 Follow the instructions on pages 8-9 to fuse all the motifs onto the appliqué fabrics, then cut the shapes. Fuse the motifs onto the background fabric, using the photograph as a guide; wind the tape measure ribbon around the sewing machine motif before fusing the appliqué. Buttonhole stitch around all the motifs, following the instructions on page 9.

2 With right sides facing, sew the two pieces together for the pincushion, and each pocket and block, leaving a 1" opening. Clip the corners, turn, and press. For Pocket E and the pincushion, clip the inward point of the curved top before turning. Stuff the pincushion, and slipstitch the opening closed. Buttonhole stitch across the top edge of each pocket, and all edges of Pocket E only. Set aside the pincushion, Pocket E, and Blocks A and F.

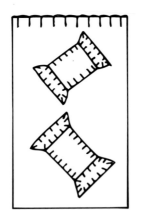

Position the pockets (omit Pocket E) on the caddy's front,

using the schematic as a guide. Buttonhole stitch around the sides and bottom, securing the pockets.

3 For Block F, place a pin every 2½" on the elastic. With a pencil, mark a line every 1½" on the block fabric. Match the pins with the pencil marks, then topstitch the elastic in place.

Use a satin stitch if you have one on your machine, otherwise straight stitch up and down on the marked lines twice. Position Blocks A and F on the caddy's front fabric and buttonhole stitch around the edges.

4 With raw ends matching, fold the ribbon lengths in half, forming the loop hangers. Pin and baste the hangers evenly across the top right side of the backing, matching the raw edges.

5 With right sides facing, pin the caddy front and the backing together and place on top of the batting. Stitch around the edges, leaving a 4" opening. Trim the excess batting, clip the corners, and turn. Slipstitch the opening. Buttonhole stitch around the edges.

6 Place the monofilament thread in the top of your machine (the thread may be too slick to use in the bobbin). Topstitch around the sides and bottom of each pocket about ¼" in from the edge. You will be stitching through five layers.

7 Position Pocket E on the caddy front. Slide your scissors under the pocket to help mark placement. The scissors' blades will emerge from the bottom of the pocket. When you are satisfied with the placement, topstitch the sides only to secure the pocket. Add pincushion to Pocket D.

8 Using the photograph as a guide, decoratively arrange the buttons. Add the buttons following the instructions on page 7.

Button Bracelet

Jackie Erickson designed this bracelet. We planned it to complement the sewing caddy, since both make wonderful gifts. You might consider using pearl or black buttons and gold safety pins—there are many possibilities. It is also a great project for children.

Supplies Needed

- Safety pins: one hundred ½"-1" safety pins
- Buttons: one hundred small or shank ½" buttons
- Elastic: 12" of round cording

Instructions

1 Wrap the elastic to fit loosely around your wrist. Tie one end into a knot. String the safety pins on the elastic. Open the pins, add the buttons, then close the pins. Tie the elastic ends together. If needed, adjust the elastic knot, then trim the knot tails.

Sewing Kit or Eyeglass Case

This fold-up sewing kit holds needles, scissors, and thread. It is nice to have next to you where you hand sew, or take it along to your quilt group. If you want an eyeglass case, simply stitch up the sides. This case makes a great gift for a quilting friend. The finished size is 6¾" x 10".

Supplies Needed

You may use the colors in the original project, but feel free to substitute with your own choices.

- Lining and backing: two 8" x 12" rectangles
- Appliqué motifs: scrap fabrics for hearts
- Thin batting: 8" x 12" rectangle
- Felt: 9" x 12" rectangle (omit for eyeglass case)
- Paper-backed adhesive: 2" x 4" rectangle
- Velcro®: 1" square
- Embroidery floss: a variety of colors totaling 1 skein

Cutting Guide

- Lining, backing, and batting: cut one each, following the pattern instructions.
- Pocket and needle book (from the felt): cut one 2¾" x 5½" rectangle for the pocket, cut one each 2½" x 6", 2½" x 5", and 2½" x 4" rectangle for the needle book

Tracing Guide

Trace two small heart appliqué shapes onto the paper-backed adhesive.

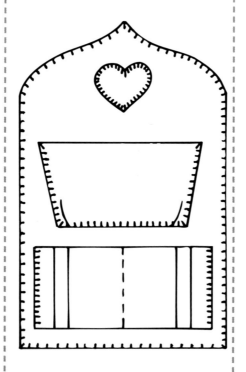

Sewing Kit or Eyeglass Case

Sewing Instructions

Use ¼" seam allowance.

1 Follow the instructions on pages 8-9 to fuse the motifs onto the appliqué fabrics, then cut the shapes. Fuse a heart motif onto the lining and backing, using the photos as guides. Buttonhole stitch around the motifs following the instructions on page 9.

2 With right sides facing, pin the lining and the backing together and place on top of the batting. Stitch around the edges, leaving a 4" opening. Trim the excess batting, clip the corners, and turn. Slipstitch the opening closed. Buttonhole stitch around the edges.

3 Take a ¼" tuck in the bottom corners of the pocket, place the pocket on the lining, and tack. Machine stitch the bottom and sides of the pocket, stitching through all layers. Position and layer the felt pieces for the needle book on the lining, starting with the largest piece on the bottom. Topstitch through the middle of the stacked felt, machine-stitching through all layers. Buttonhole stitch the bottom and sides of the pocket, and the sides of the bottom felt piece, stitching through one layer of fabric only.

4 Fold the sewing kit in thirds with the flap overlapping the bottom fold. Position the Velcro under the flap, and secure to the fabric.

Optional: tie a ribbon end to the handle of your scissors, then tack the other end to the sewing kit.

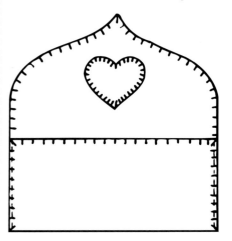

5 For an eyeglass case, omit step 3, and fold up the bottom, then stitch the sides together.

small spool

heart pincushion

small heart

leaf for large pincushion

needle

top of large spool

large spool

bottom of large spool

pocket E

43

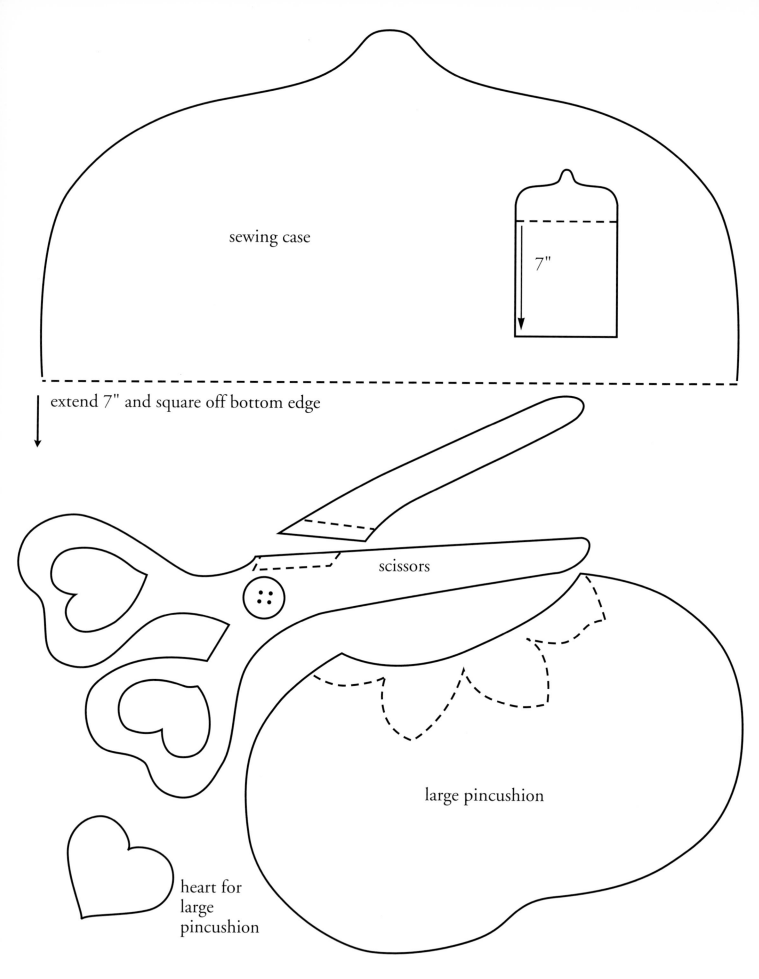

sewing case

7"

extend 7" and square off bottom edge

scissors

large pincushion

heart for large pincushion

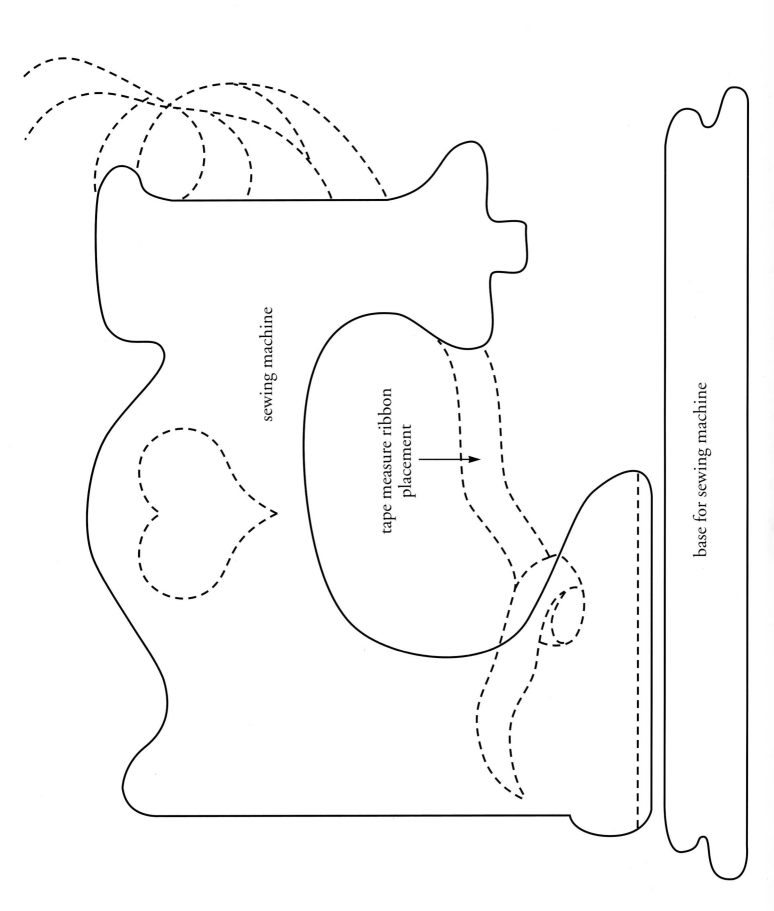

sewing machine

tape measure ribbon placement

base for sewing machine

Stitches & Spools Patterns

Trellis Fans Quilt

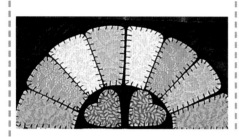

The four-wedge fan within the center blocks are appliquéd instead of pieced. The floral fabric for the block background creates the feeling of a flowing vine garden. The border fan blocks combined with the trellis vine blocks accent the theme of the quilt. Marina Anderson, a friend and graphic artist, drew the fan and vine border for an ad in my store 15 years ago—her designs continue to inspire me! The finished size is 44½" x 44½".

Supplies Needed

You may use the colors in the original project, but feel free to substitute with your own choices.

- Blocks A, F, G: 1⅓ yards
- Blocks B, E: ½ yard
- Blocks C and D, binding, and vines (bias strips): 1 yard
- Appliqué motifs: ⅓ yard each of four coordinating colors for fan wedges, ⅓ yard for hearts and leaves
- Backing: 1⅔ yards
- Batting: 47" x 47"
- Paper-backed adhesive: 4 yards
- Embroidery floss: a variety of colors totaling 5 skeins

Cutting Guide

- Block A: cut four strips 8½" x 42". From the strips cut sixteen 8½" squares.
- Block B: cut two strips 4½" x 42". From the strips cut eight 8½" rectangles.
- Block C: cut two strips 4½" x 42". From the strips cut eight 8½" rectangles.
- Block D: cut one strip 4½" x 18". From the strip cut four 4½" squares.
- Block E: cut one strip 4½" x 18". From the strip, cut four 4½" squares.
- Block F: cut two strips 2½" x 32½".
- Block G: cut two strips 2½" x 36½".

- Binding: cut four strips 1¾" x 42" and one 1¾" x 21". Stitch the short edges of the strips together. From the long strip, cut two strips 45" for the top and bottom, and two strips 44½" for the sides.
- Backing: cut one piece 42" x 47", one 5½" x 42", and one 5½" x 5½". Join the two strips into one long strip. Trim off the selvages and stitch the two sections together, right sides facing.

Tracing Guide

Trace the following appliqué shapes onto the paper-backed adhesive:

- Blocks A: 64 large fan wedges, 16 large hearts
- Blocks B: 32 leaves, eight small circles
- Blocks C: 64 small fan wedges, 16 small hearts
- Blocks D: 16 small fan wedges, four small hearts
- Blocks E: eight leaves, four hearts

Trellis Fans Quilt

Sewing Instructions

Use ¼" seam allowance.

1 Follow the instructions on pages 8-9 to fuse all the motifs onto the appliqué fabrics, then cut the shapes. Fuse the motifs onto the background fabric for Blocks A, C, and D. Keep a ¼" seam allowance remaining around the edge of the block. Buttonhole stitch around all the motifs following the instructions on page 9.

2 Using the schematic as a guide, stitch four each Blocks A together to form four rows. Join the rows together to make the quilt center.

3 For the border, add a Block F to the top and bottom, and a Block G to each side of the quilt center, following the instructions on page 10.

4 To form the vines for Blocks B and E, cut bias 1⅛" wide strips to total 236". Stitch the bias strips together to form one long piece.

Fold the strip in half length-wise, with wrong sides facing, and press.

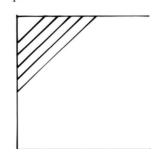

Referring to the patterns on pages 52-53, transfer the vine placement lines onto Blocks B and E. Match the raw edge of the bias strip to the marked line of the vine. Stitch the strip ⅛" to ³⁄₁₆" from the raw edge to secure. Fold the pressed edge over the seam, then slipstitch in place to cover the raw edge. For Block B, finish stitching the first vine strip, before you add the second vine strip. Fuse the remaining motifs onto the background fabric for Blocks B and E. Buttonhole stitch around the motifs.

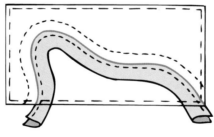

The circle motifs are held in place with a cross stitch: come up

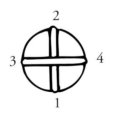

from the fabric back at 1, go down at 2, come again at 3, and go down again at 4. Secure the thread tails.

5 Using the schematic as a guide, stitch the border blocks together in the following sequence: Block B to C to E to C to B. Stitch a Block D each to an end of two strips for the top and bottom borders. Following the border instructions on page 10, add the side strips first, then the top and bottom strips.

6 Using the vine outline pattern from Block B, transfer for quilting lines, ignoring seams where the blocks join and between the diagonal rows of fan wedges in the quilt center. The quilting lines in the border blocks outline the shapes of the motifs. Finish the quilt according to the instructions on page 10.

Grandma's Memories Picture Frame

These picture frames are great gifts for grandmas. Flowers from the large print fabric used in the *Trellis Fans* quilt are fused to the corners of this picture frame. To add interest and inspiration, buttonhole stitching outlines the flower clusters, window opening, and the edges of the frame. The finished size is 9" x 12".

Supplies Needed

You may use the colors in the original project, but feel free to substitute with your own choices. The example is a purchased 9" x 12" pre-cut mat frame (the front has a 5½" x 8½" window opening, the back is solid). Make adjustments to the supplies if you choose a different size. You can easily adjust a square or rectangle window for the frame.

- Frame front and back: ⅓ yard (two coordinating fabrics can be used instead of one)
- Appliqué motifs: scrap fabric
- Thin batting: 10" x 13" rectangle
- Paper-backed adhesive: 6" x 9" rectangle
- Embroidery floss: two coordinating colors totaling 1 skein
- Frame base: 9" x 12" pre-cut mat
- Hot-glue gun or craft glue

Cutting Guide

- Frame back: cut two 9½" x 12½" rectangles
- Frame front: cut one 10" x 13" rectangle

Grandma's Memories Picture Frame

Sewing Instructions

1 Using ³⁄₁₆" seam allowance and with right sides facing, sew the two backs together, stitching the sides and bottom only. Clip the corners, turn, and press. Slip the back mat between the fabrics. Turn the raw edges inside and slipstitch the opening.

2 Place the front mat (with window opening) on the wrong wide of the front fabric. With a pencil, trace around all edges. Trim the window opening to within ¾" of the traced line. If it is an oval, clip every ½" to within ⅛" of the traced line.

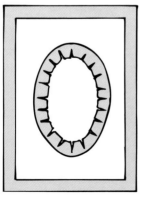

3 Place the front mat on the batting and mark the edges with a felt pen. Trim the batting on the marked line.

4 Using the flowers from a large print, fuse a piece of adhesive over the fabric design, then cut around the shapes. Fuse them on the right side of the frame front. Buttonhole stitch around the flower edges following the instructions on page 9.

5 Place the right side of the front fabric on a table, then layer with the batting and place the front mat on top. Align the edges with the pencil marked lines. Pull the clipped fabric tabs over the edge of the window opening (so the marked lines are at the edge of the cardboard) and glue down. Work the opposite side, then the top and bottom. Once these are secure, finish gluing the remaining tabs. If you are using craft glue, it will be necessary to hold the newly glued area with a clothespin until the glue is dry.

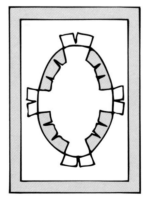

6 Glue the outside edges in the same manner—opposite sides, then top and bottom. Using the illustration as a guide, work the fabric to each corner. Pull the fabric ends up at the corners, then fold them down in a wedge and glue.

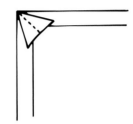

7 Buttonhole stitch around the window opening and the frame's outer edges. Position the frame back piece on the wrong side of the frame front. Whipstitch the two together, leaving an opening at the top to insert a picture.

Sewing Instructions

1 Cut around the flower motif edges. On mine I left a little of the black background, so it outlines the shape. I was going to buttonhole stitch around the motifs, but the flowers are pretty intricate and it would look too busy. If your flowers are more of a simple shape, the stitching would work better.

2 Place the ribbon for the band on the hat, then cross the ends at the center back, leaving two tails. Notch the ribbon ends. With needle and thread, tack the ribbon in place.

3 With the wire-edge ribbon, start working at the side of the hat crown, crinkling and twisting the ribbon, creating the feeling of "little nests." If you look closely at the photograph, you will see areas where the ribbon is flatter and areas where it is crunched. The ribbon is very forgiving so you can rework it if you need to. Just remember you are creating a feeling of "texture."

4 Look for a place where the silk ribbon wraps around the crown that is a little off center. Arrange the clusters of fused flowers to cover the odd spots. Play with these, adding them to the ribbon work. Stand back and observe your creativity!

5 When you like it, tack it in place. Optional embellishments might be little buttons or beads, or narrower ribbons could be tucked under the clusters of flowers. Have fun with your hat decorating.

Sunny Days Straw Hat

The purchased hat is decorated with silk and taffeta ribbons, a silk flower, and fused fabric flowers. The colors were chosen to complement the *Trellis Fans* quilt, but any floral fabric could be used in the same manner. The natural charm of the straw hat inspires thoughts of sunny days and summer picnics.

Supplies Needed
You may use the colors in the original project, but feel free to substitute with your own choices.
- Purchased hat
- Ribbon for band: use 1" to 1⅝"-wide ribbon, then measure around the crown and add 12" to the length.
- Wire-edge ribbon: 1 yard of 1⅝"-wide ribbon
- Silk flower to complement your fabric colors
- Floral fabric: scraps or ⅛ yard of fabric with large printed flowers
- Paper-backed adhesive: ⅛ yard

Tracing Guide
- Isolate the flower shapes you want to cut around, then cut the adhesive slightly larger. Following the instructions on page 8, fuse the adhesive to the wrong side of the cut flowers. You will need enough for three groupings (at least nine flowers). Peel off the paper backing and fuse again to the leftover fabric, creating a two-sided flower.

large fan wedge

small heart

large heart

small fan wedge

Block E

trace leaves
& heart

Block B

trace leaves &
small circle

2

1

vine

Wings of Romance Quilt

The *Wings of Romance* quilt has a romantic, nostalgic fabric color palette, accented with pieces of lace, ribbons, cording, and buttons. This quilt could just as easily be made from bright jewel tones. The simplicity of the appliqué design lends itself to many possibilities. The finished size is 27½" x 39½".

Supplies Needed

You may use the colors in the original project, but feel free to substitute with your own choices.

- Blocks A: ½ yard
- Blocks B, C, D, E: ⅛ yard each of four coordinating colors
- Appliqué motifs: assorted scraps totaling 1 yard
- Lace: I used two and one half 8" Battenburg doilies, pieces of three other doilies, three 6"pieces of flat trim, and the corner of one hanky. Look at what you already have, then use my quilt as a starting point, making your own lace collage.
- Ribbon: depending on your lace choices, pick ribbons that can lay beside the lace or be worked through it. I like wire-edged ribbon because I can crinkle it and make it dimensional. You can fold or stitch ¼"-wide ribbon into loops. Gather up a palette of ribbons that complement the colors in the fabric. If you are collecting ribbons, buy 1 yard cuts.
- Cording: 1¼ yard
- Binding: ¼ yard
- Backing: 1 yard
- Batting: 30" x 42" rectangle
- Paper-backed adhesive: 1½ yards
- Embroidery floss: a variety of colors totaling 3 skeins

Cutting Guide

- Blocks A: cut two strips 8½" x 42". From the strips, cut eight 10½" rectangles.
- Block B: cut a 4" x 32½" rectangle
- Block C: cut a 4" x 24" rectangle
- Block D: cut a 4" x 36" rectangle
- Block E: cut a 4" x 27½" rectangle

- Binding: cut four strips 1¾" x 42". From the strips, cut two strips 28" for the top and bottom, and two 39½" strips for the sides.
- Backing: cut a 30" x 42" piece

Tracing Guide

Trace the following appliqué shapes onto the paper-backed adhesive:

- Blocks A: eight hearts, eight sets of wings (a set consists of a right side and a left side)

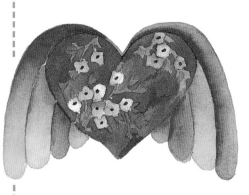

Wings of Romance Quilt

Sewing Instructions

Use ¼" seam allowance.

1 Follow the instructions on pages 8-9 to fuse all the motifs onto the appliqué fabrics, then cut the shapes. Fuse the motifs onto the background fabric for each block. Center the wings first, then add the heart motif. Keep a ¼" seam allowance remaining around the edge of the block. Buttonhole stitch around all the motifs following the instructions on page 9.

2 Stitch four each Blocks A into two vertical rows. With right sides facing, join the two rows, forming the quilt center. Buttonhole stitch around each block except for the raw edges.

3 Arrange the border blocks around the quilt, then pin the laces and ribbons on each strip to make a collage. The laces are placed first, then the ribbons are next, and the buttons top it off. If you look closely at the photograph, you can see the layering. To make ribbon loops, fold the ribbon in half, matching the ends, and tack. You may want to double or triple the loops. Loops add dimension and texture if you make them peak out from under the button clusters.

4 Follow the instructions on page 7 to add the buttons. To overlap buttons, bring the needle up beside the edge of the last button, then add the next one. The second one will automatically overlap the first. Vary the size of the buttons in the cluster, letting a couple trickle out from the others to create a "stream". Flip the buttons to find other possibilities. Sometimes the back side of old pearl buttons will be rougher in texture and have a more interesting color.

5 When I first start embellishing with ribbons and buttons, I don't have an end plan in mind. I set the stage with the lace, then let the ribbons and buttons grow. With me, one idea leads to another and I have to have my needle in hand to start getting ideas.

6 The hankie and lace glove were added after the border blocks were stitched. For the border blocks, add Block B then add C, D, and E, following the instructions on page 10. After the borders are added, buttonhole stitch around the outer edges of the quilt center.

7 Machine quilt in the ditch, then "doodle quilt" in all the background areas. To start doodle quilting, place a piece of tissue over the area to be quilted. Start drawing from an inward point of the heart, or on the lace, and come out and make a curve. Repeat the curve, varying the width of the lines and circle at the end. Once you have practiced on paper, you can lightly pencil the lines on the quilt. Pretty soon you will be doodle quilting free hand. Finish the quilt according to the instructions on pages 10-11.

Quilter's Keepsake Journal

I like to keep journals of my quilting and garden experiences, so I thought it would be fun to sew my own journal. The cover is the winged heart motif from the Wings of Romance quilt. Padded poster board inside the cover gives the journal a soft sculptured look. The finished size is 7½" x 11½".

Supplies Needed

You may use the colors in the original project, but feel free to substitute with your own choices.

- Journal front and back: ¼ yard each of two coordinating fabrics (one for the covers and one for the lining)
- Appliqué motifs: scraps for the heart and wings
- Posterboard: 12½" x 14½" rectangle
- Note paper: twelve to twenty 7¼" x 11½" sheets
- Thin batting: 8" x 24" rectangle
- Ribbon: ½ yard of narrow wire edge
- Paper-backed adhesive: ¼ yard
- Embroidery floss: coordinating colors totaling one skein

Cutting Guide

- Cover: cut two 8" x 14" rectangles
- Lining: cut two 8" x 14" rectangles
- Batting: cut two 7³⁄₁₆" x 11³⁄₁₆" rectangles
- Posterboard: cut two 7³⁄₁₆" x 11³⁄₁₆" and two 1¼" x 7³⁄₁₆" rectangles.

Tracing Guide

Trace a heart and a set of wings (left and right) on paper-backed adhesive.

Quilter's Keepsake Journal

Sewing Instructions

1 Follow the instructions on pages 8-9 to fuse the motifs onto the appliqué fabrics, then cut the shapes. Fuse the motifs onto the cover fabric, using the illustration as a guide. Center the wings first, then add the heart motif. Buttonhole stitch around all the motifs following the instructions on page 9.

← 12" →

2 For the front cover, place a lining piece over the right side of the cover. Stitch three sides together, leaving the edge for the left side open. Clip the corners, turn, and press. Repeat for the back cover.

3 Glue the batting pieces to the posterboard pieces at the corners.

4 Insert the posterboard into the covers, with the batting side facing the cover fabric. Machine stitch about ⅛" from the edge of the posterboard, through all the layers as shown below.

↖ *stitching line*

5 Using a hole punch, punch a hole in 1¼" on each end of the remaining posterboard strips.

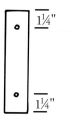

1¼"

1¼"

Transfer the hole markings onto a sheet of paper. Stack the paper and punch the holes. Insert the posterboard pieces into the sewn sleeve on the covers. Turn in the raw edges of the fabric and slipstitch the opening.

6 Insert the paper between the two covers. Make sure no paper is sticking out at left end of the book when you fold the covers over the paper. Align the holes in the covers (covered by the fabric)

inside front cover   *paper*

with the holes in the paper. Using a large embroidery needle with two strands of thread, insert the needle into one hole, through the fabric, to the cover back. Insert the needle into the other hole in the same manner, and continue working the thread to bind the journal.

Using the photo as a guide, make a simple flat bow with the wire edge ribbon, and tack on the inside binding. Buttonhole stitch around the edge of the journal.

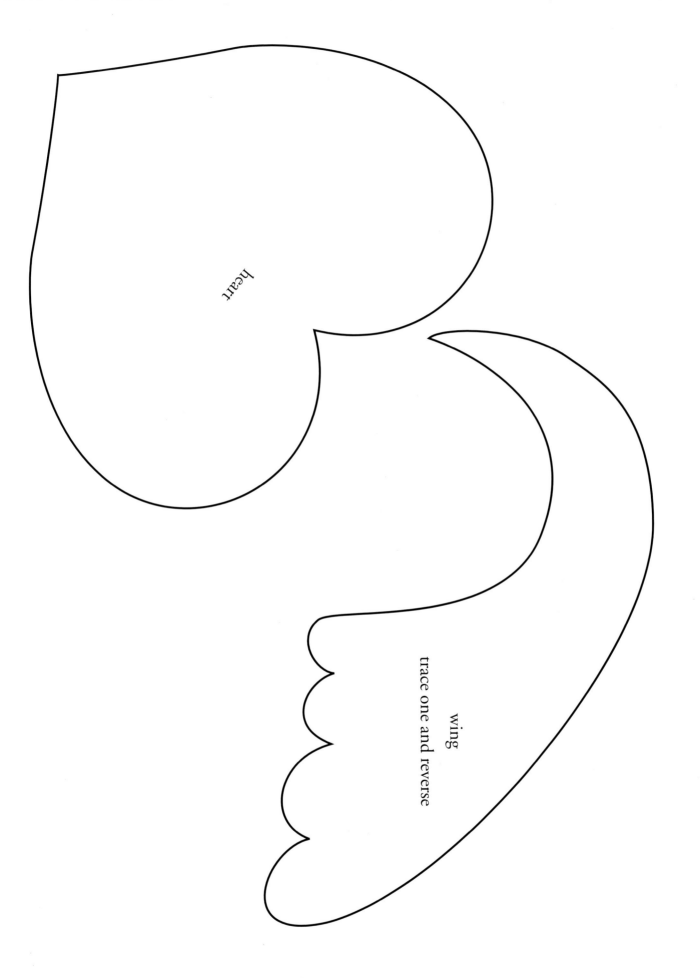

heart

wing
trace one and reverse

Wings of Romance Patterns

Wild Hare in the Garden Quilt

Next to quilting, gardening is my favorite pastime. Planting a garden is like quilting—you have to wait for the final results. My garden quilt started out with the wild hare leaping over the carrots and expanded from there. The dimensional flowers were an experiment that worked, and add a real life effect to the quilt. Your garden might be a fall garden, or a cityscape, instead of a country plot. Your choice of fabrics will create an individual mood for your garden. The finished size is 44½" x 48½".

Supplies Needed

You may use the colors in the original project, but feel free to substitute with your own choices.

- Blocks A and B: two 8½" x 11½" rectangles
- Block C: 5½" x 16½" rectangle
- Block D: 6½" x 16½" rectangle
- Block E: 5" x 22½" rectangle
- Blocks F, I, and K: 1 yard of sky-blue fabric
- Block G: 3" x 7½" rectangle
- Block H: 6½" x 22½" rectangle
- Blocks J, L, M, and binding: 1 yard
- Block N: ¼ yard
- Border inset: ⅛ yard
- Appliqué motifs: ⅛ yard for the fence, ¼ yard each for the sunflower stem, roof, and leaves, and a variety of scraps totaling 2 yards for the remaining motifs
- Buttons: 19 assorted buttons for flower centers
- Backing: 1⅞ yards
- Batting: 47" x 51" rectangle
- Paper-backed adhesive: 4 yards
- Embroidery floss: coordinating colors totaling 3 skeins

Cutting Guide

- Blocks A, B, C, and D are pre-cut
- Blocks E: cut two 2½" x 22½" rectangles
- Block F: cut one 7½" x 20½" rectangle
- Blocks G: cut two 1½" x 7½" rectangles
- Block I: cut one 9½" x 22½" rectangle
- Block J: cut two 6½" x 8½" rectangles
- Blocks K: cut two 8½" x 36½" rectangles
- Block L: cut two 3½" x 42½" strips
- Block M and N: cut a strip 3½" x 42" and one 3½" x 4". Piece the strips together and cut to 44½" for the top and bottom borders.
- Border inset: cut three 1" x 42½" strips. Trim one strip to 38½". If your fabric is not 42½" wide, piece the strips together.
- Binding: cut five strips 1¾" x 42". Piece the strips, then cut two strips 45" for the top and bottom and two strips 48½" for the sides.
- Backing: cut a 42" x 47" rectangle, a 9½" x 42" strip, and a 9½" x 5½" strip. Join the strips together. Trim off the selvages and sew the two sections together, with right sides facing.

Tracing Guide

Trace the following appliqué shapes onto the paper-backed adhesive:

- Block A: two vines, 11 leaves, three pea pods, seven flower petals
- Block B: one pot, three tulips and stems, four leaves
- Block C: one star flower vine, 12 star flower leaves, six star flowers
- Block D: two radishes with leaves
- Block F: one wild hare and six carrot tops
- Block H: six carrots
- Block I: two birds, 20 flower petals, ten leaves, roof (see step 2)
- Blocks J: six fence posts, eight connectors
- Blocks K: one sunflower, one stem, five leaves, one birdhouse, one medium heart, one star, vines with 11 leaves, 20 flower petals, three birds, one wild hare, 1" x 14" pole

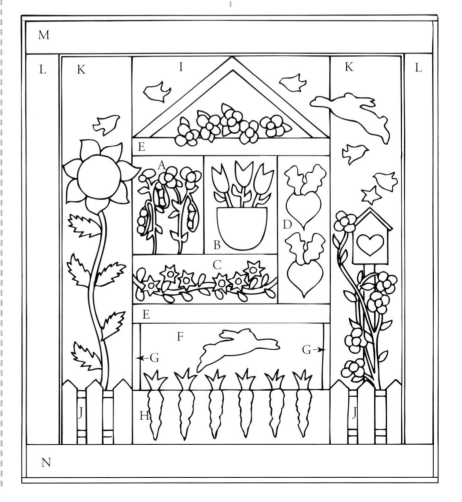

Wild Hare Quilt

Sewing Instructions

1 Follow the instructions on pages 8-9 to fuse all the motifs onto the appliqué fabrics, then cut the shapes. The wild hare in the right-hand corner, the right sunflower petal, the carrots and the fence are added after the adjacent blocks are sewn together.

2 For Block I, cut a piece of adhesive 7½" x 18" for the roof. Fold it in half, short edges together. Using a ruler, mark a diagonal line from the lower left corner to the top right corner (at the center fold). Cut on the line and you have the roof pattern. Fuse to the roof appliqué fabric and cut the shape. Position the roof appliqué on Block I, centering along the bottom edge,

[diagram: rectangle labeled 7½" and 18"]

and lightly press in place.

For the roof trim, cut two strips of adhesive 1½" x 14½" and fuse to the appliqué fabric. Overlap the edges at the roof peak until they are ¼" from the top of the background fabric. Trim the ends off to match the block.

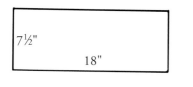

3 There are dimensional flowers on the peas, the stems along the birdhouse, and in the roof. To make the flowers, fuse two pieces of fabric together, following the instructions on page 8. Trace and cut around the petal shape. Buttonhole stitch around the edge. Repeat for the roof's leaves. With needle and thread, take a small tuck at the base of the flower petal. It will curl up just like a real petal. Add three or four together to form a flower.

Fuse the remaining motifs onto the background fabric for each block. Buttonhole stitch around all the motifs following the instructions on page 9. On the narrow stems buttonhole stitch across the whole stem.

4 Stitch the blocks together. The sequence of block construction follows the letters given to the blocks. Before adding Block F, stitch a Block G to each end, with right sides facing and matching the edges. Add a Block J to a Block K before stitching to the quilt center.

5 Fold the border insets in half lengthwise and press. Matching raw edges, baste the 38½"-long inset on the top and the other two insets on the sides of the quilt center, matching the raw edges. After the blocks are sewn, the border inset will show ¼" of the folded fabric, forming a tiny accent border.

6 Following the border instructions on page 10, stitch a Block L to each side of the quilt center. Add Blocks M and N to form the top and bottom borders. Tack the dimensional flowers in place. Stitch a button in the center of each flower.

7 Machine quilt in the ditch in the seam lines and outline quilt around the appliqué motifs. Finish the quilt according to the instructions on page 10.

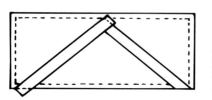

Gardening Shirt

I found a lightweight denim shirt, with black and white accent striping, to decorate with gardening motifs. When you plan the appliqués, first put the shirt on, then think about where you want the eye to be drawn. I used multiple colors of floss and buttonhole stitched around the collar and down the front band. I replaced the buttons to make them match the appliqués.

Supplies Needed

- Purchased shirt
- Appliqué motifs: scraps for all of the appliqués
- Paper-backed adhesive: 1 yard
- Embroidery floss: coordinating colors totaling 2 skeins
- Optional buttons: if replacing the original buttons

Tracing Guide

Trace the following appliqué shapes onto the paper-backed adhesive:

- large sunflower with three leaves and stem, three carrots and tops, two stars, one wild hare, and radish with leaves.

Sewing Instructions

1. Follow the instructions on pages 8-9 to fuse all the motifs onto the appliqué fabrics, then cut the shapes. Fuse the motifs onto the shirt, using the photograph as a guide. Buttonhole stitch around the motifs, the collar, and down the front band. Optional: replace the front buttons.

Gardening Hat

Dimensional, buttonhole-stitched tulips and daisies decorate the brim of this purchased cotton hat. Buttons are added for the flower centers.

Supplies Needed

- Purchased cotton hat with brim
- Appliqué motifs: a variety of scraps totaling ¼ yard for flowers, scraps for leaves
- Buttons: four assorted 1"-wide buttons for flower centers
- Paper-backed adhesive: ¼ yard
- Embroidery floss: one skein

Tracing Guide

Trace the following appliqué shapes onto the paper-backed adhesive:

- three tulips, petals for four daisies, and six leaves.

Sewing Instructions

1 Follow the instructions on pages 8-9 to fuse all the motifs onto the appliqué fabrics, then cut the shapes. Follow the instructions in step 3 of *Wild Hare in the Garden* quilt to make the dimensional flowers and leaves.

2 Arrange the flowers and leaves on the hat brim, and tack in place. Stitch a button in the center of each daisy, following the instructions on page 7.

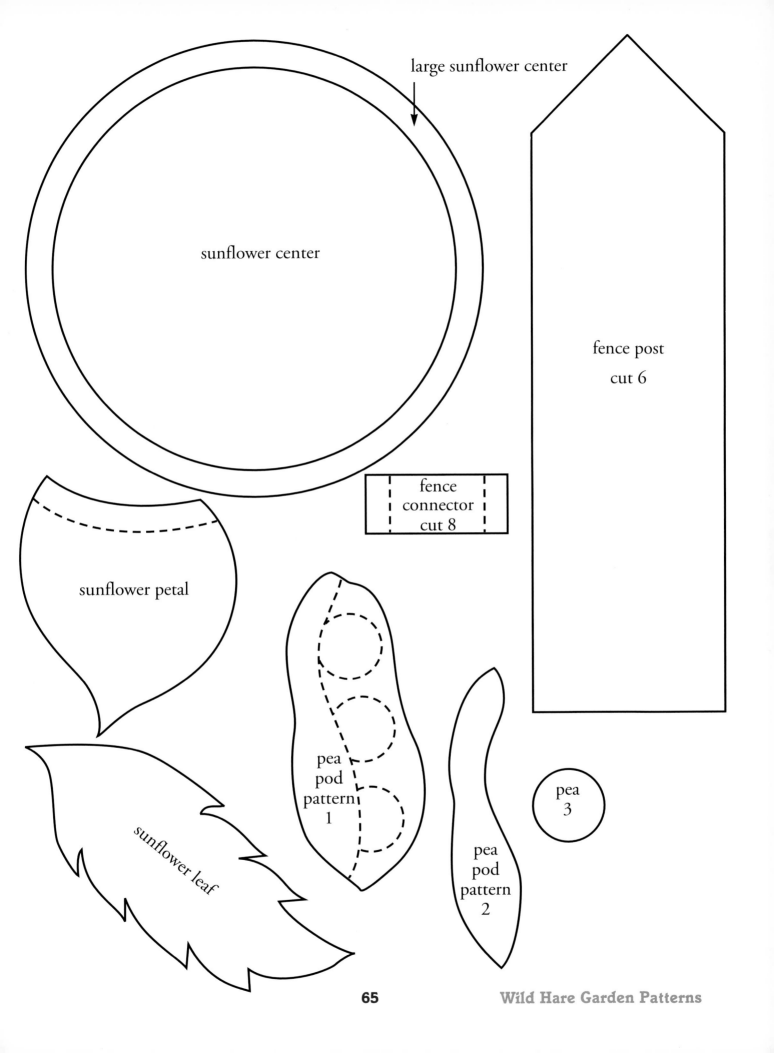

large sunflower center

sunflower center

fence post
cut 6

fence
connector
cut 8

sunflower petal

pea
pod
pattern
1

pea
pod
pattern
2

pea
3

sunflower leaf

Wild Hare Garden Patterns

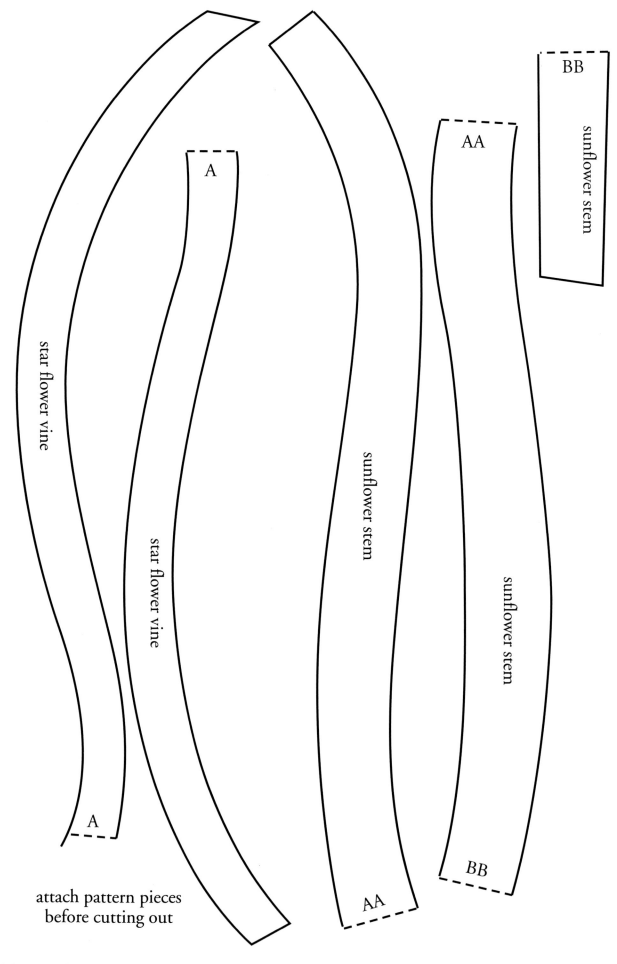

BB

sunflower stem

AA

A

star flower vine

star flower vine

sunflower stem

sunflower stem

A

AA

BB

attach pattern pieces
before cutting out

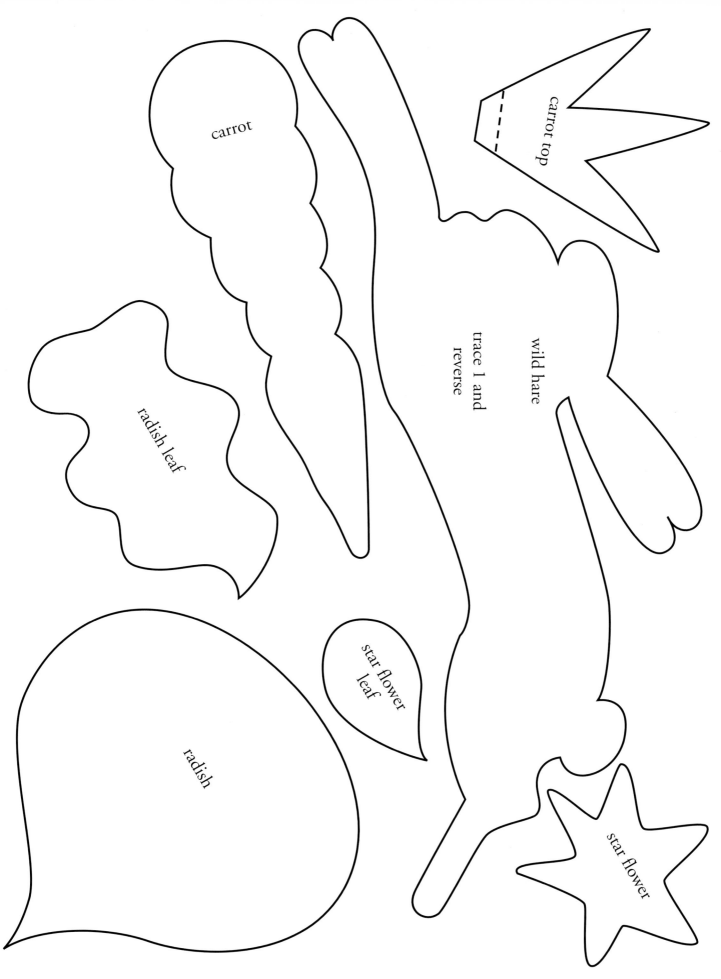

carrot

carrot top

wild hare

trace 1 and
reverse

radish leaf

radish

star flower
leaf

star flower

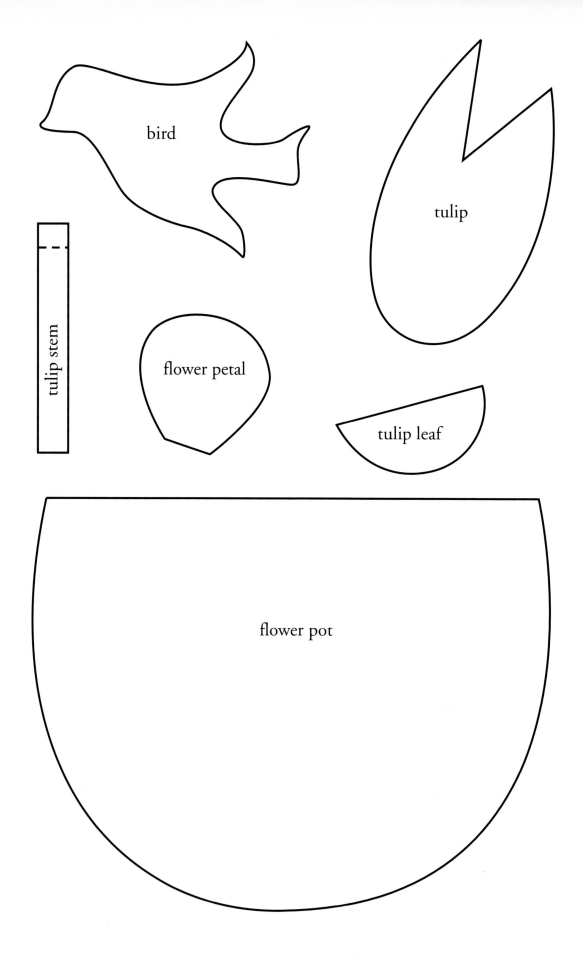

bird

tulip

tulip stem

flower petal

tulip leaf

flower pot

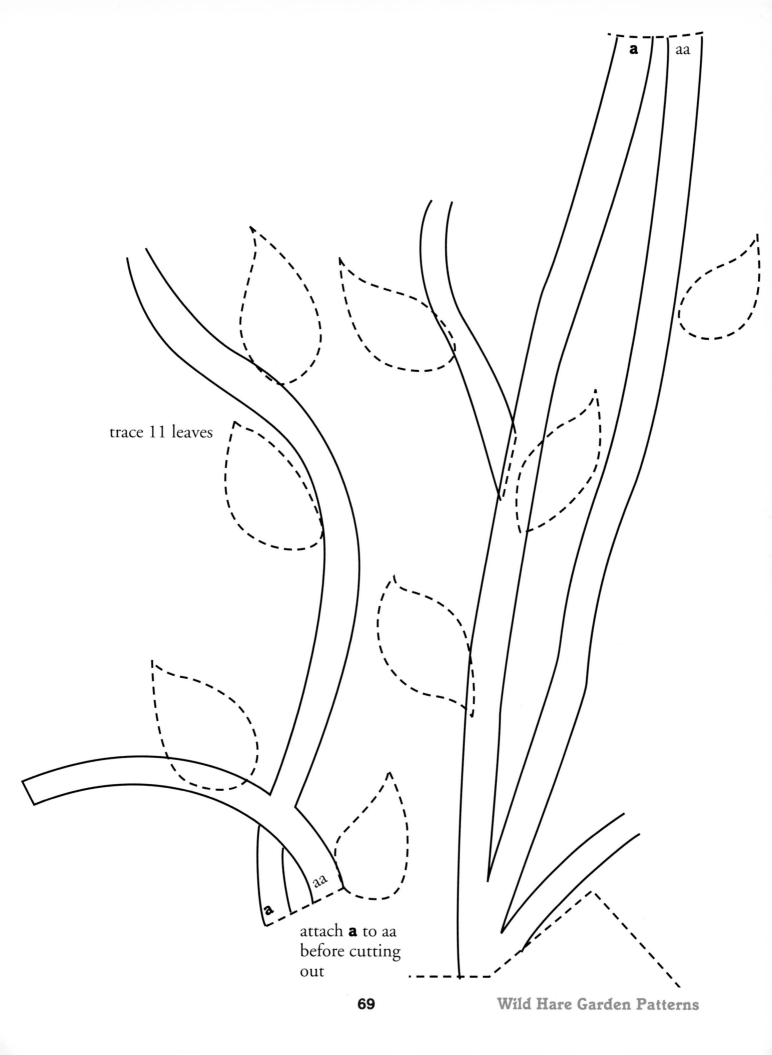

trace 11 leaves

a   aa

aa

a

attach **a** to aa
before cutting
out

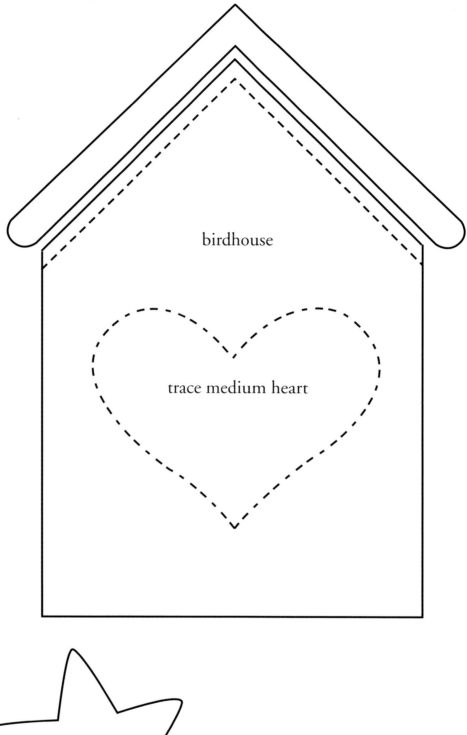

birdhouse

trace medium heart

star

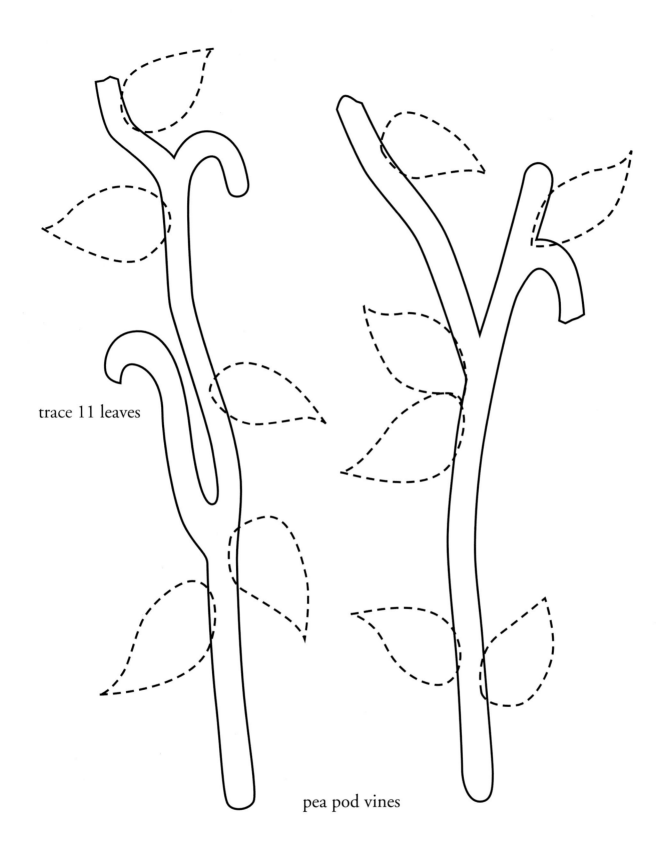

trace 11 leaves

pea pod vines

Baskets & Fans Quilt

As I designed this quilt, a soft pink and green palette just seemed to work together. There are corners of white hankies under the fan appliqués. Andrea Balosky hand quilted around the design, repeating the diagonal lines of the central medallion. It is stitched with a slightly brighter pink thread than the fabric, adding an accent and repeating the pink in the hearts. The finished size is 27½" x 27½".

Supplies Needed

You may use the colors in the original project, but feel free to substitute with your own choices.

- Blocks A and E: ¼ yard
- Blocks B, D, and binding: ¾ yard
- Blocks C: two 9⅞" squares
- Appliqué motifs: ⅛ yard each of four coordinating pinks and three greens, scrap of dark pink
- Hankies: four 12" hankies with two matching corner designs
- Backing: ⅞ yard
- Batting: 30" square
- Paper-backed adhesive: 2 yards
- Embroidery floss: 2 skeins

Cutting Guide

- Blocks A and E: cut eight 5" squares
- Blocks B: cut two 7¼" squares, then cut the squares in half diagonally
- Blocks C: cut two 9⅞" squares, then cut the squares in half diagonally
- Blocks D: cut two strips 5" x 42". From the strips cut four 18½" rectangles
- Binding: cut four strips 1¾" x 42". From the strips cut two strips 28" for the top and bottom, and two strips 27½" for the sides.
- Backing: cut a 30" square

Tracing Guide

Trace the following appliqué shapes onto the paper-backed adhesive:

- Blocks A: four each basket patterns 1-3
- Blocks B: 16 fan wedges
- Blocks C: four sets of Log Cabin patterns 1-7
- Blocks D: 16 fan wedges
- Blocks E: four each basket patterns 1-3

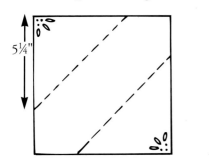

Baskets & Fans Quilt

Sewing Instructions

Use a ¼" seam allowance.

1 Follow the instructions on pages 8-9 to fuse the motifs onto the appliqué fabrics, then cut the shapes. Measure down the sides of each hanky 5¼", then cut diagonally. Repeat until you have eight triangles.

Position the hankies on Blocks B, matching the raw edge of the

hankies to the long edges of Blocks B. Mark the midpoint of Blocks D, and center the hanky on Block D with the raw edges matching. Buttonhole stitch the hankies before adding the small fan wedges. Fuse the fan motifs onto the hankies. Buttonhole

stitch around the fans following the instructions on page 9.

2 For Blocks C, position the Log Cabin pieces on the background fabric. Leave the ¼" seam allowance on the two short sides of the triangle. Fuse the pieces onto the background fabric.

Buttonhole stitch around the motifs following the instructions on page 9.

3 Refer to the schematic for the block placement. To form the quilt center, stitch four Blocks A together, using the schematic as a guide. Add a Block B to each side, then add a Block C to each side. For the border, add a Block D to the top and bottom following the instructions on page 10. Stitch a Block E to each end of the remaining D blocks and add to the sides of the quilt center.

4 Machine stitch in the ditch between the block sections, and hand quilt around the appliqué shapes. The quilted grid lines in Blocks D are 1" apart. Finish the quilt according to the instructions on page 10.

Teddy Bears

These simple shaped teddy bears are outlined with buttonhole stitching. The bear is 7½" tall. You could easily enlarge the pattern and make a mom, dad, or cubs. The samples show two bears of cotton fabric. The third one is of Warm and Natural® batting. It was the easiest to stitch because the edges don't unravel.

Supplies Needed

The listing is for one teddy bear.

- Bear fabric: ¼ yard
- Eyes: ⅛" black beads
- Nose: 12" black floss
- Stuffing: approx. 6 oz
- Ribbon: ⅓ yard of 2"-wide ribbon for bow
- Embroidery floss: 1 skein

Cutting Guide

- Cut the teddy bear pattern pieces.

Sewing Instructions

Use ¼" seam allowance.

1 For the face, place the pieces together, with right sides facing, and stitch from points A to B. Clip at point B and back tack. Open the face and match to the head back, with wrong sides facing. Stitch around the head, from point C to C. The seam allowances are on the outside and will be decorated with buttonhole stitches later.

2 Place the body pieces together, with wrong sides facing, and stitch around the body from points D to D.

3 Place each arm together, with wrong sides facing, and stitch around the arms from points E to E.

4 Stuff the head, body, and arms. Trim off any excess raveling at the fabric edges before you buttonhole stitch. Following the instructions on page 9, buttonhole stitch around each piece, except for the top of the body and the bottom of the head.

5 Tuck the neck of the body into the top of the head, then whipstitch firmly in place.

6 Sew the beads on for eyes. Use six strands of embroidery floss to work the nose, stitching across the top of the nose four to six times and using the photo as a guide for placement.

7 Using a large needle, attach the thread to the X on one arm. Go through the body and attach at the other arm. Weave the needle through the body several times and knot the thread end securely.

8 Tie a ribbon bow around the teddy bear's neck.

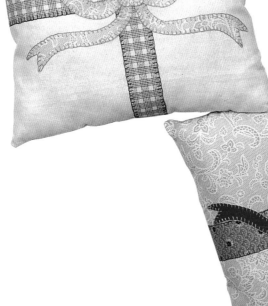

Cutting Guide
- Pillow front and back: cut two 12½" squares

Tracing Guide
Trace the following appliqué shapes onto the paper-backed adhesive:
- one bow, two 1½" x 12½" strips for the ties

Sewing Instructions
Use ¼" seam allowance.

1 Follow the instructions on pages 8-9 to fuse the motifs onto the appliqué fabrics, then cut the shapes.

2 Cross the ties on the pillow top, matching the ends to the fabric edge, and fuse in place. Decoratively position the bow and fuse in place. Buttonhole stitch around all the motifs following the instructions on page 9.

3 Place the pillow front and back together, with right sides facing. Stitch around the edges, leaving a 5" opening for turning. Clip the corners, turn, and press. Fill with stuffing, and slipstitch the opening.

Bow Pillows

Ribbon and bow shapes decorate these square pillows. The ribbon ties were buttonhole stitched first, then the bow shapes. On the green pillow, the bow is at an angle, and on the white pillow, the bow is straight—you can choose your favorite. You could change the pillow shape for variety. The finished size is 12" x 12".

Supplies Needed
The listing is for one pillow.
- Pillow fabric: ⅜ yard
- Appliqué motifs: ⅛ yard each for ties and bow
- Paper-backed adhesive: ¼ yard
- Embroidery floss: two coordinating colors totaling 2 skeins
- Stuffing: 12 oz.

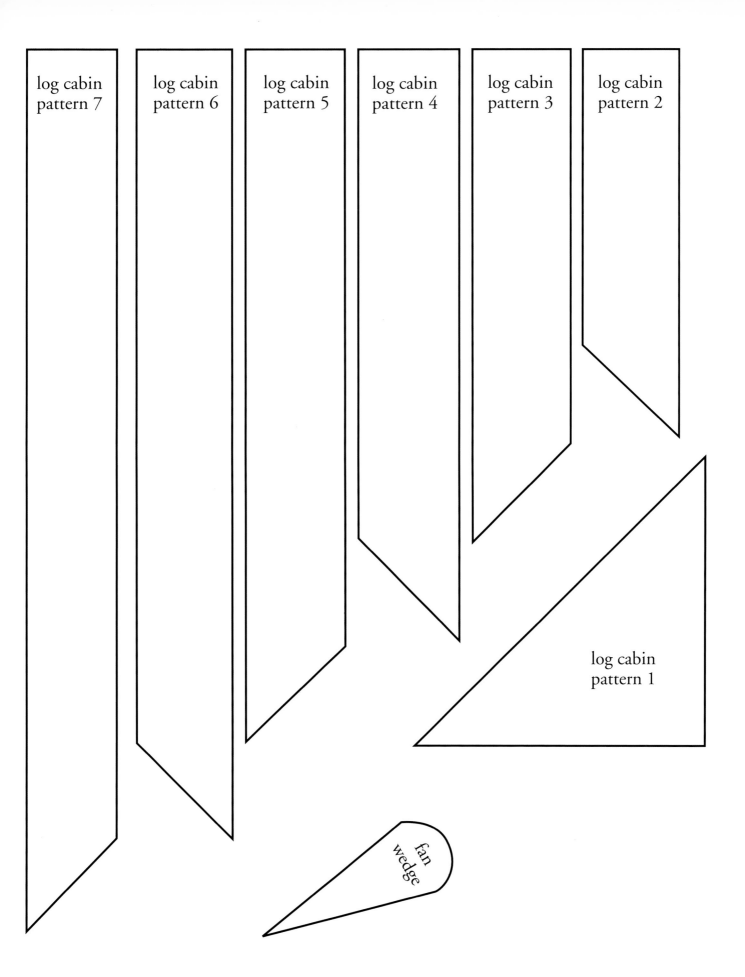

log cabin
pattern 7

log cabin
pattern 6

log cabin
pattern 5

log cabin
pattern 4

log cabin
pattern 3

log cabin
pattern 2

log cabin
pattern 1

fan
wedge

Baskets & Fans Patterns

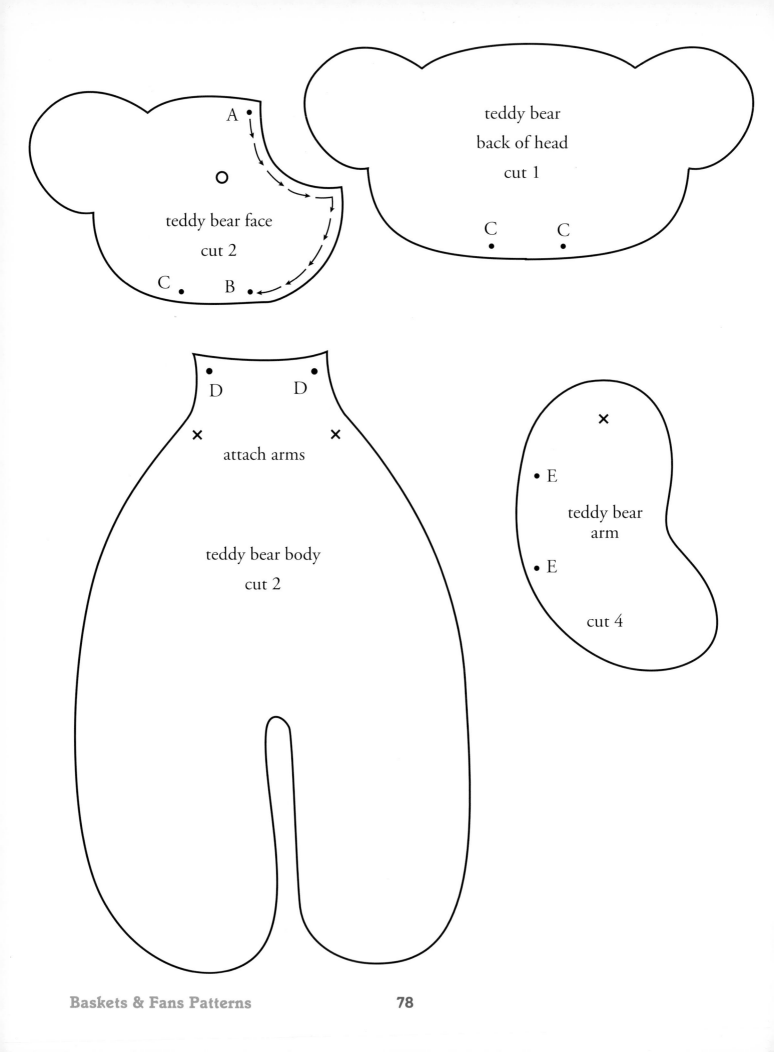

A

O

teddy bear face
cut 2

C   B

teddy bear
back of head
cut 1

C   C

D   D

✕   attach arms   ✕

teddy bear body
cut 2

✕

• E

teddy bear
arm

• E

cut 4

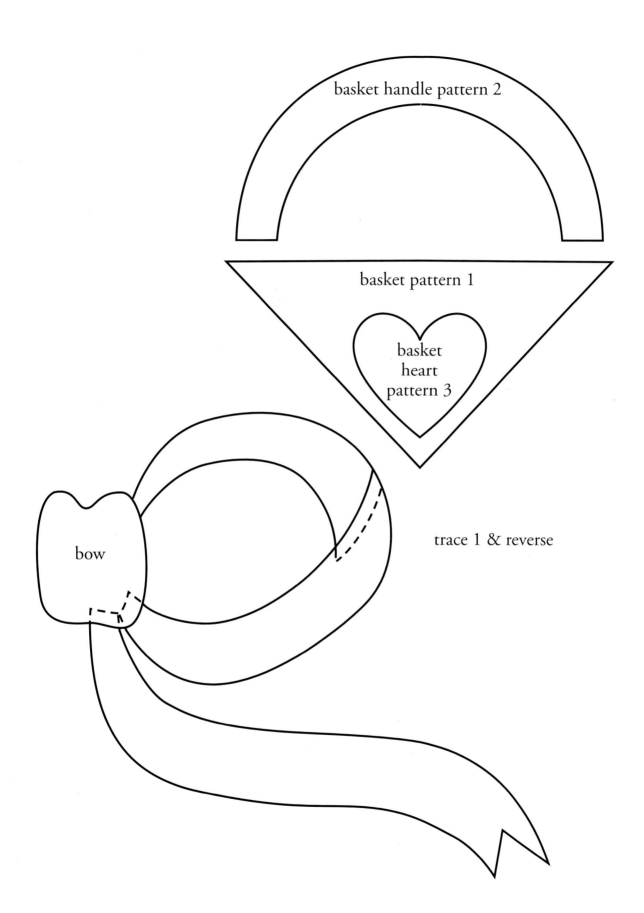

basket handle pattern 2

basket pattern 1

basket
heart
pattern 3

bow

trace 1 & reverse

Angelic Christmas Banner

Within the banner, the star points radiate out from the heart, adding a feeling of celebration and excitement to the design. The star points are repeated in the border, and this adds a whimsical touch to the banner. Note the differences in color from the same heart on the front cover. You can easily project a different mood by changing the colors within the design. The colors in this banner use the "echo" technique. The hot pink echoes the red, the lime green the medium green, and the yellow the gold. This technique works well when your values are close in the major pieces of a banner. Finished size is 18" x 28¼".

Supplies Needed

Colors are named in the supply list only to assist you in selecting colors that echo each other—feel free to substitute with your own choices.

- Banner background: ⅝ yard of blue
- Appliqué motifs and border: ½ yard red for heart, wings, and border, ½ yard pink for heart, wings, apron and border, ¼ yard green for trees and border, 9" square lime green for heart and apron trim, 8" square medium green for heart, and apron trim, ⅛ yard yellow for wing's stars, ⅓ yard gold for large star, star points, tubs, dress, headpiece, and border hangers, ⅛ yard light blue for circles, ⅛ yard purple for star points and apron trim, scrap of brown for tree trunks, scrap of muslin for face and feet
- Backing: ⅝ yard
- Batting: 18½" x 25½" rectangle
- Paper-backed adhesive: 2 yards
- Embroidery floss: coordinating colors totaling 2 skeins
- Fray Check®
- Black and red permanent pens

Cutting Guide

- Background, backing, and batting: cut one each 18½" x 25½" rectangle
- Border strips: two 2" x 18" strips of red, two 1½" x 18" strips of pink and two 1" x 18" strips of green
- Loops: cut one 2" x 12" strip

Tracing Guide

Trace the following appliqué shapes onto the paper-backed adhesive

- four alpine trees, one angel with wings and stars, center motifs (refer to step 1 in the sewing instructions).

Angelic Christmas Banner

Sewing Instructions

Use ¼" seam allowance.

1 Photocopy the heart pattern and tape the two pieces together. Remember you have the left side only. Fold a 12½" x 15½" piece of paper-backed adhesive in half. Trace the pink outline heart, with the edge along the fold. Repeat for the other three hearts.

Trace an extra ¼" on the inside edge of the pink outline large heart, as indicated by the dashed line. Then when you layer the hearts, the red heart will overlap the extra ¼" allowance.

Number the star points for placement purposes. You will need two each of the points. Trace all of the points, and extend each ¼" as

indicated by the dashed line on the pattern. If you place two pieces of adhesive right sides together before cutting, you will have points for the left and right sides.

You will also need two each of the circles. Number them and cut as you did the points. Fuse the motifs onto the appliqué fabric and cut the shapes.

2 Center the pink outline heart 11¼" down from the top of the background fabric. After the pink outline heart is in place, keep adding the motif layers until you get to the large star. Slip the edge of the points under the lime heart. Lightly press each piece, and after all the pieces are in place, fuse the pieces following the manufacturer's instructions.

3 Draw a face on the angel before fusing it in place. Center the angel's dress above the heart. The angel patterns allow for overlapping. Lightly press each piece as you layer, and after all the pieces are in place, fuse the pieces following the manufacturer's instructions.

4 Fuse the trees in the tubs on both sides of the appliqués. Trace six each large and small star border points on the adhesive for the bottom of the border. Fuse the motifs onto the appliqué fabric and cut the shapes. Cut six large border star points from the fabric (for the back), fuse together, then add the smaller point on top. Buttonhole stitch all the motifs.

5 Fold each border strip in half lengthwise and press. Put Fray Check® on the raw edges at the end of the strips. Layer the strips, starting from the bottom and matching the raw edges (red, pink, green). Stitch the layers together ¼" from the edge.

6 Place the wrong side of the banner on top of the batting. Place the borders on the top and bottom. Pin together, with the green strip facing down and the raw edges matching. On the bottom edge, arrange the star points with right sides facing the banner. Stitch through all of the layers.

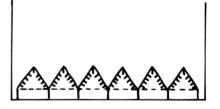

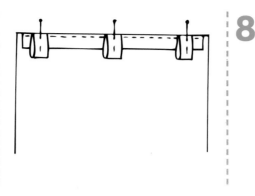

7 Fold the loop hanger strips in half lengthwise, with right sides facing, and stitch ¼" from the raw edge. Turn to the right side. Cut the strip into three 4" lengths and press. Fold the loop hanger strips in half and place evenly apart on the banner top, then pin in place.

8 Place the right side of the backing on the right side of the banner. Using ¼" seam allowance, stitch the sides and the top, leaving the bottom open. Clip the excess at the corners. Turn to the right side. At the banner bottom, turn under the edge of the backing and stitch in place.

Angel Doll

Lawry Thorn constructed this doll; the angel motif on the banner was the design basis for the angel doll. Display the doll with a doll stand, or add it to decorate a wreath or tree. It also makes a delightful gift for a little girl. If you want a larger doll, simply enlarge the patterns on a photocopy machine. The finished size is 10½".

Supplies Needed

You may use the colors in the original project, but feel free to substitute with your own choices.

- Doll body: ¼ yard of muslin
- Dress: ¼ yard
- Apron: 6" x 8" rectangle
- Wings: 7" x 20" rectangle
- Appliqué motifs: scraps
- Lightweight batting: 7" x 10" rectangle
- Stuffing: 8 oz.
- Ribbon: ⅝ yard of ⅛"-wide ribbon for apron ties
- Hair: 2½" of roving, or small amount of yarn
- Paper-backed adhesive: ⅛ yard
- Permanent pen
- Black craft paint for shoes
- Embroidery floss: 1 skein

Cutting Guide

- Dress: cut two 2½" x 2" pieces for the bodice, two 4" squares for the sleeves, two 7½" x 9" pieces for the skirt
- Apron: cut two 1¾" x 1¾" pieces for the bib, one 5" x 7" piece for the skirt
- Wings: cut two of fabric and one of batting
- Ribbon: cut two 8" and two 1½" lengths

Tracing Guide

Trace the following appliqué shapes onto the paper-backed adhesive:

- trim for apron, four stars for wings

Sewing Instructions
Body

Use ¼" seam allowance.

1 Cut the patterns. Fold the muslin in half so you will be working with two layers of fabric. Trace one body, two arms, and two legs on the muslin, leaving ¼" around the edges for the seam allowance.

2 Using a small stitch (16 stitches to the inch) stitch the arms and legs on the traced lines, through both layers of muslin. Do not stitch across the tops of the arms and legs. Cut the arms and legs from the muslin, leaving a ³⁄₁₆" seam allowance. Turn to the right side. Firmly stuff the arms to within 1" of the shoulder, and the legs within 2" from the top.

3 Cut the body pieces from the muslin, but do not stitch first. Place the legs at the bottom of one body, matching the raw edges. Stitch across the legs.

Trace the shoe outlines onto the body front. With right sides facing, stitch the bodies together at the sides and around the head, leaving the bottom open. Turn to the right side.

4 Stuff the head and body tightly. Turn under the raw edge at the bottom of the body and slipstitch the opening.

5 Fold under the raw edges of the arm ends. Pin the ends to body front, then zigzag stitch in place.

6 Paint the shoes on the bottom of the legs where you marked them. Let the paint dry thoroughly before you dress the doll. Wait to paint the face and add the hair until you have completely dressed the doll.

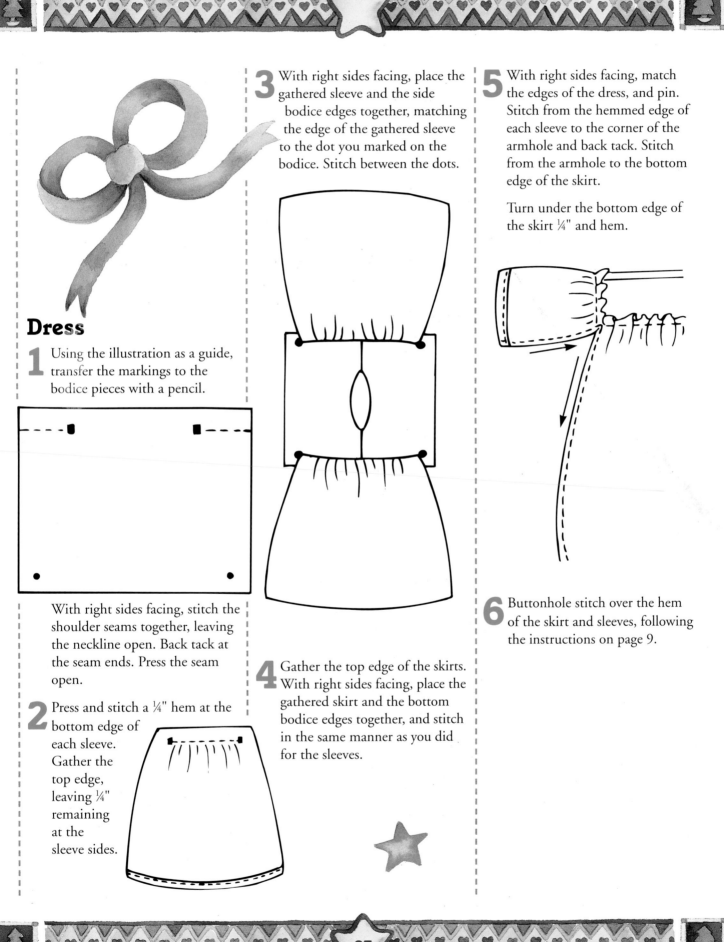

3 With right sides facing, place the gathered sleeve and the side bodice edges together, matching the edge of the gathered sleeve to the dot you marked on the bodice. Stitch between the dots.

5 With right sides facing, match the edges of the dress, and pin. Stitch from the hemmed edge of each sleeve to the corner of the armhole and back tack. Stitch from the armhole to the bottom edge of the skirt.

Turn under the bottom edge of the skirt ¼" and hem.

Dress

1 Using the illustration as a guide, transfer the markings to the bodice pieces with a pencil.

With right sides facing, stitch the shoulder seams together, leaving the neckline open. Back tack at the seam ends. Press the seam open.

2 Press and stitch a ¼" hem at the bottom edge of each sleeve. Gather the top edge, leaving ¼" remaining at the sleeve sides.

4 Gather the top edge of the skirts. With right sides facing, place the gathered skirt and the bottom bodice edges together, and stitch in the same manner as you did for the sleeves.

6 Buttonhole stitch over the hem of the skirt and sleeves, following the instructions on page 9.

Apron

1 Turn under the sides and bottom edge of the apron ¼" and hem. Gather the top edge.

2 With right sides facing, stitch the gathered skirt and the bib edge together, leaving ¼" of the bib edge remaining on each side.

3 Place the ribbons on the right side of the bib. Make a little loop out of the shorter ribbons for each of the sides. Pin in place.

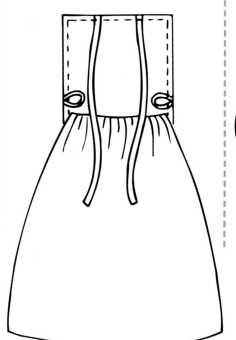

Place the right side of the remaining bib piece over the bib section and stitch the three outer edges. Turn to the right side. Turn under the bib's raw edge and slipstitch to the apron back.

4 Follow the instructions on pages 8-9 to fuse the trim motifs onto the scrap fabric, then cut the shapes. Fuse the trim onto the apron fabric. Add buttonhole stitching around the skirt and apron edges, and the apron trim.

5 Dress the doll. To tie the apron, cross the ribbon ties on the doll's back and slip through the side loops. Tie the ribbon ends in the back.

Wings

1 Place the wing pieces together, with right sides facing, then pin to the lightweight batting. Stitch together, using ⅛" seam allowance. You may use a ¼" seam allowance if you choose, but the wings will be slightly smaller. Make a slit through one layer of the fabric.

Clip at the inward point of the heart. Turn and press the edges lightly. Whipstich the opening closed.

2 Fuse four stars to the slit side of the wings. It will be stitched next to the body. Buttonhole stitch around the edge of the stars. Slipstitch the wings to the doll's back.

Face and Hair

1 Using the permanent pen, mark the face. You may want to use a cotton swab and add a tiny bit of blush to her cheeks.

2 Cut a piece of roving 2½" long and unravel slightly. Tack to the head. Option: use a small piece of gold elastic or wire and make a halo.

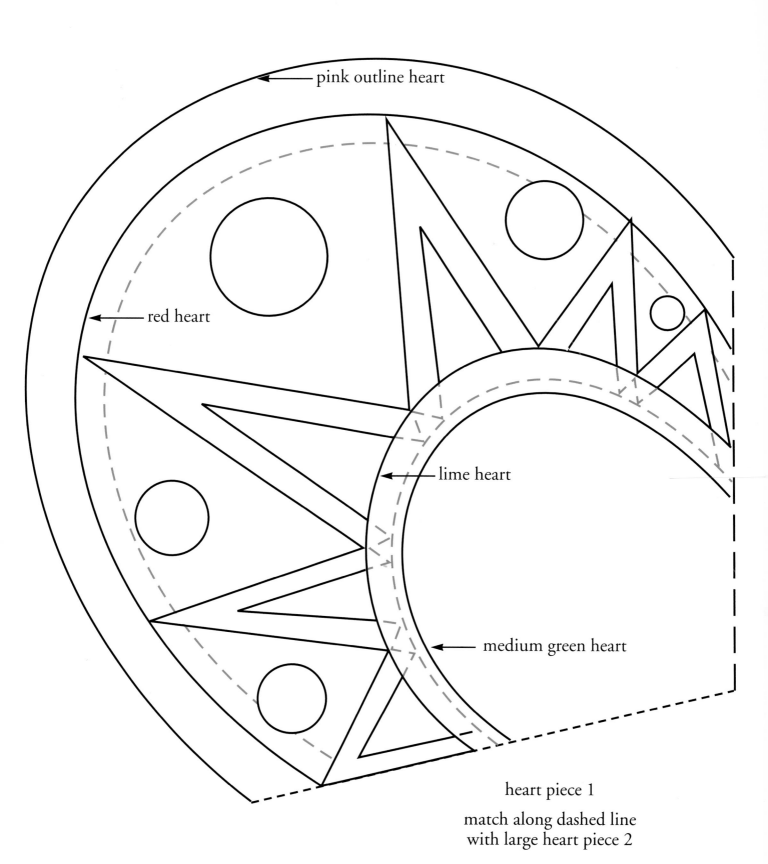

pink outline heart

red heart

lime heart

medium green heart

heart piece 1

match along dashed line
with large heart piece 2

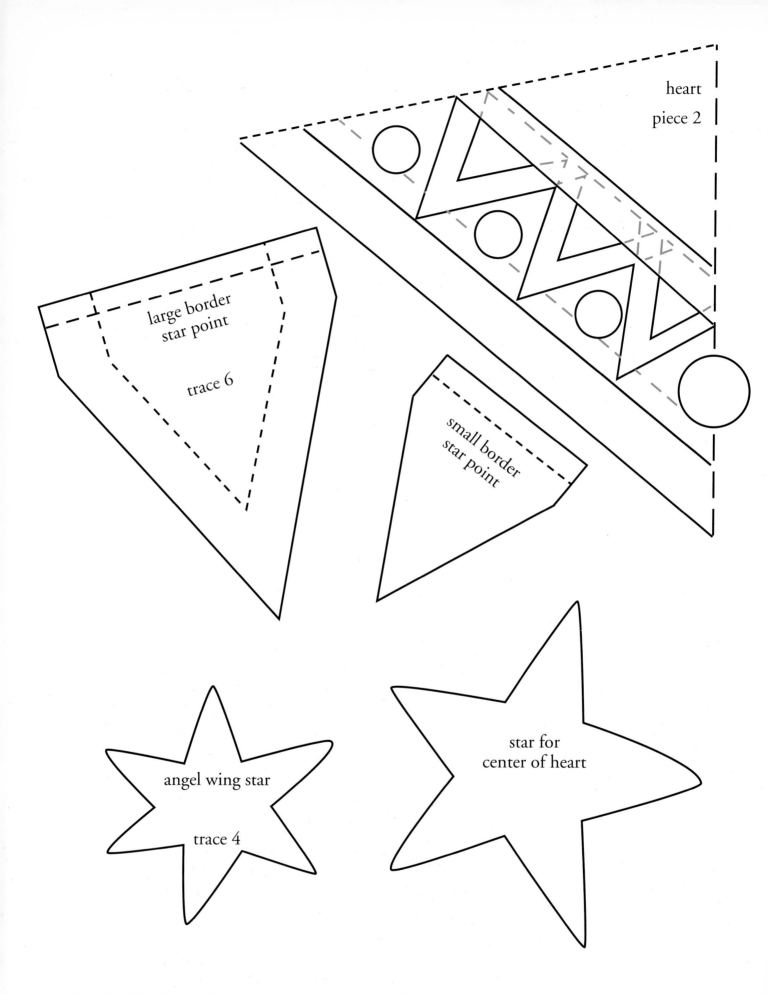

heart
piece 2

large border
star point

trace 6

small border
star point

star for
center of heart

angel wing star

trace 4

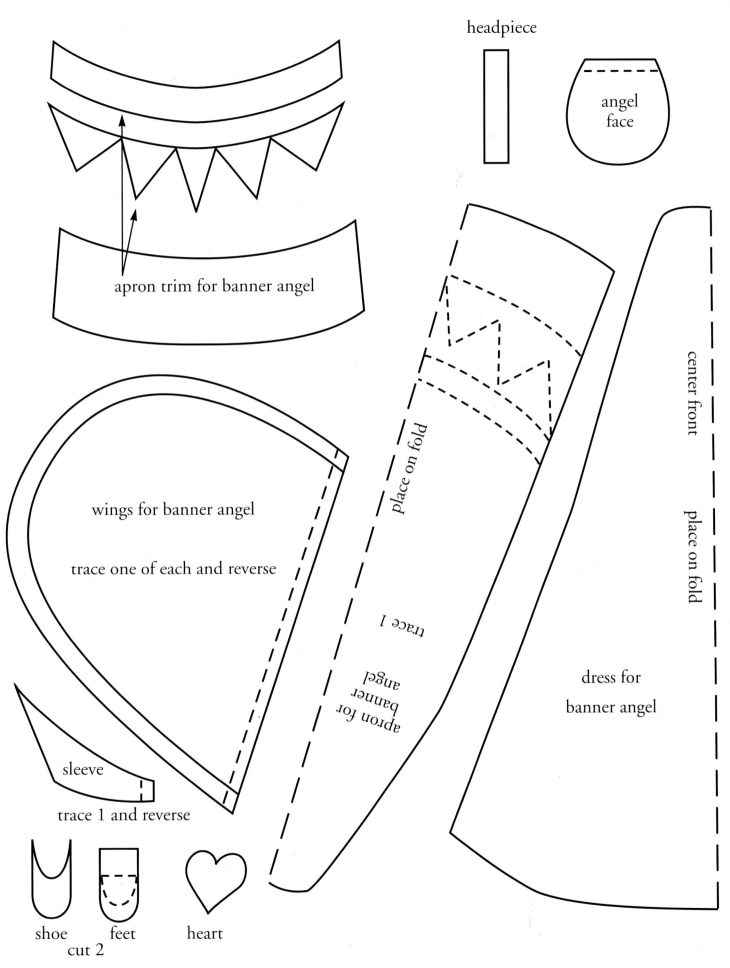

headpiece

angel face

apron trim for banner angel

wings for banner angel

trace one of each and reverse

place on fold

trace 1

apron for banner angel

center front

place on fold

dress for banner angel

sleeve

trace 1 and reverse

shoe

feet
cut 2

heart

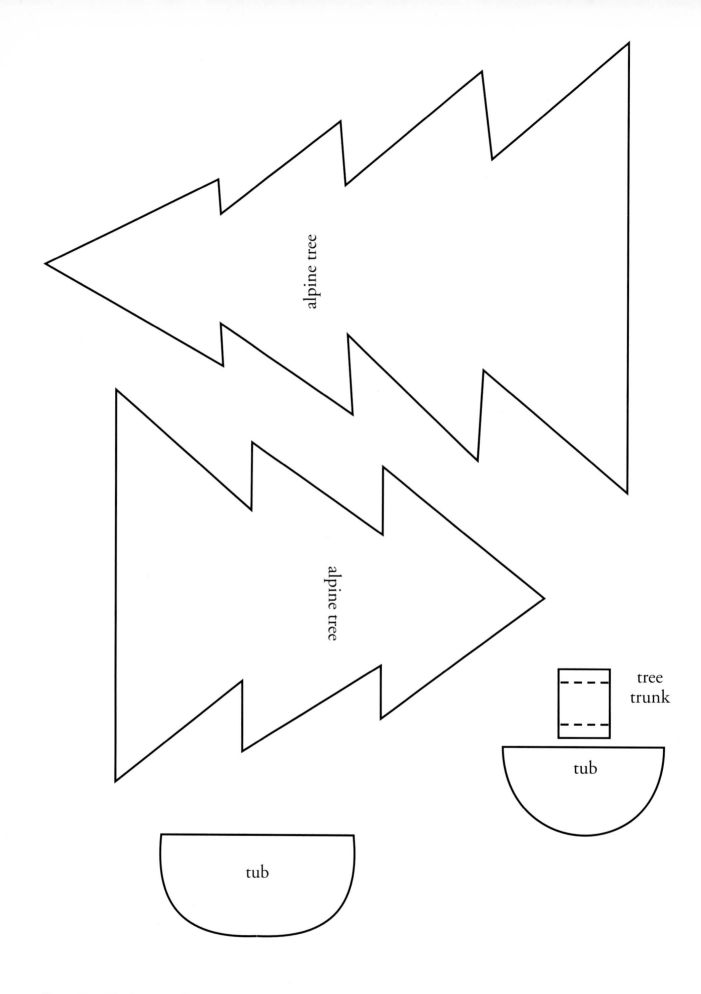

alpine tree

alpine tree

tree trunk

tub

tub

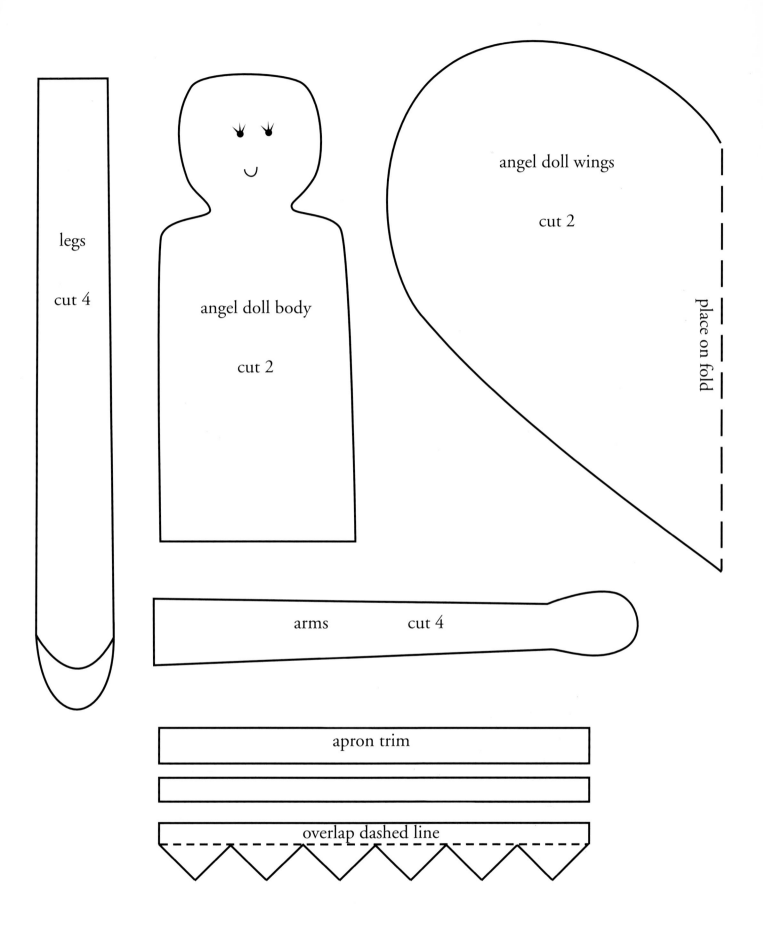

legs

cut 4

angel doll wings

cut 2

place on fold

angel doll body

cut 2

arms   cut 4

apron trim

overlap dashed line

About the Author

Jean Wells' fascination with fabric and design continues in her latest book *Buttonhole Stitch Appliqué*. She is not satisfied with one style of quilting, but likes to develop new ideas in her classes that later turn into published works. Her love of fabric, and everything that has to do with quilting, is evident in her retail store, The Stitchin' Post, located in the little mountain community of Sisters, Oregon.

Jean continues to teach quilt making on a national level, as well as in her store. She has been in the quilting business for 20 years. Her devotion to the industry is evident in her instruction of business seminars to fellow quilt-shop retailers.

Jean contributes articles to various quilting publications, and does freelance design for McCall's Patterns and Fabric Traditions. Her Fairfield Fashion Show garments are always a treat. On a more personal level, she and her husband live in the country, surrounded by mountains and a rustic garden that she tends herself. Both of her children are in college.

Books by Jean Wells

A Celebration of Hearts, Jean Wells and Marina Anderson
Memorabilia Quilting, Jean Wells
NSA Series: Bloomin' Creations, Jean Wells
NSA Series: Holiday Magic, Jean Wells
NSA Series: Hometown, Jean Wells
NSA Series: Fans, Hearts, & Folk Art, Jean Wells
PQME Series: Basket Quilt, Jean Wells
PQME Series: Bear's Paw Quilt, Jean Wells
PQME Series: Country Bunny Quilt, Jean Wells
PQME Series: Milky Way Quilt, Jean Wells
PQME Series: Nine-Patch Quilt, Jean Wells
PQME Series: Pinwheel Quilt, Jean Wells
PQME Series: Sawtooth Star Quilt, Jean Wells
PQME Series: Stars & Hearts Quilt, Jean Wells
Patchwork Quilts Made Easy, Jean Wells (co-published with Rodale Press)

Other Fine Quilting Books From C&T Publishing

An Amish Adventure, Roberta Horton
Appliqué 12 Easy Ways! Elly Sienkiewicz
Appliqué 12 Borders and Medallions! Elly Sienkiewicz
The Art of Silk Ribbon Embroidery, Judith Montano
Baltimore Album Quilts, Historic Notes and Antique Patterns, Elly Sienkiewicz
Baltimore Album Revival! Historic Quilts in the Making. The Catalog of C&T Publishing's Quilt Show and Contest, Elly Sienkiewicz
Baltimore Beauties and Beyond (2 Volumes), Elly Sienkiewicz
The Best From Gooseberry Hill: Patterns For Stuffed Animals & Dolls, Kathy Pace
Boston Commons Quilt, Blanche Young and Helen Young Frost
Calico and Beyond, Roberta Horton
Christmas Traditions From the Heart, Margaret Peters
Christmas Traditions From the Heart, Volume Two, Margaret Peters
A Colorful Book, Yvonne Porcella
Colors Changing Hue, Yvonne Porcella
Crazy Quilt Handbook, Judith Montano
Crazy Quilt Odyssey, Judith Montano
Dating Quilts—From 1600 to the Present, Helen Kelley
Design a Baltimore Album Quilt! Elly Sienkiewicz
Dimensional Appliqué—Baskets, Blooms & Baltimore Borders, Elly Sienkiewicz
Elegant Stitches, Judith Baker Montano
Fantastic Figures: Ideas & Techniques Using the New Clays, Susanna Oroyan

Flying Geese Quilt, Blanche Young and Helen Young Frost
14,287 Pieces of Fabrics and Other Poems, Jean Ray Laury
Friendship's Offering, Susan McKelvey
Happy Trails, Pepper Cory
Heirloom Machine Quilting, Harriet Hargrave
Imagery on Fabric, Jean Ray Laury
Isometric Perspective, Katie Pasquini-Masopust
Landscapes & Illusions, Joen Wolfrom
Let's Make Waves, Marianne Fons and Liz Porter
The Magical Effects of Color, Joen Wolfrom
Mariner's Compass, Judy Mathieson
Mastering Machine Appliqué, Harriet Hargrave
The New Lone Star Handbook, Blanche Young and Helen Young Frost
Papercuts and Plenty, Vol. III of Baltimore Beauties and Beyond, Elly Sienkiewicz
Pattern Play, Doreen Speckmann
Picture This, Jean Wells and Marina Anderson
Pieced Clothing, Yvonne Porcella
Pieced Clothing Variations, Yvonne Porcella
Plaids and Stripes, Roberta Horton
Quilts for Fabric Lovers, Alex Anderson
Quilts, Quilts, and More Quilts! Diana McClun and Laura Nownes
Recollections, Judith Montano
Soft-Edge Piecing, Jinny Beyer
Stitching Free: Easy Machine Pictures, Shirley Nilsson
Story Quilts, Mary Mashuta
Symmetry: A Design System for Quiltmakers, Ruth B. McDowell
3 Dimensional Design, Katie Pasquini
A Treasury of Quilt Labels, Susan McKelvey
Trip Around the World Quilts, Blanche Young and Helen Young Frost
Virginia Avery's Hats, A Heady Affair
Virginia Avery's Nifty Neckwear
Visions: Quilts, Layers of Excellence, Quilt San Diego
The Visual Dance Creating Spectacular Quilts, Joen Wolfrom
Whimsical Animals, Miriam Gourley
Wearable Art for Real People, Mary Mashuta

For more information write for a free catalog from
C&T Publishing
P.O. Box 1456
Lafayette, CA 94549
(1-800-284-1114)